At the Chelsea

At the Chelsea

Florence Turner

HARCOURT BRACE JOVANOVICH, PUBLISHERS

SAN DIEGO   NEW YORK   LONDON

The frontispiece quotation is from *The Autobiography of Maxim Gorky*, translated by Isidore Schneider (New York: Citadel Press, 1949). Reprinted by permission of Citadel Press. "The Hotel Chelsea" by Edgar Lee Masters (pages 10–11) is reprinted from Hardin Wallace Masters' *Edgar Lee Masters: A Biographical Sketchbook* (Fairleigh Dickinson University, 1978). Reprinted by permission of Associated University Presses. The line from "The Emperor of Ice Cream" (page 58), copyright © 1923, renewed 1-9-1951, by Wallace Stevens, reprinted from *The Collected Poems of Wallace Stevens*, by permission of Alfred A. Knopf, Inc. The lines from "Sara" by Bob Dylan (page 61) copyright © 1975, 1976 by Ram's Horn Music. All rights reserved. International copyrights secured. Reprinted by permission. The lines from "Chelsea Hotel No. 2" (page 62) from *New Skin for an Old Ceremony* (CBS Records, 1974), copyright © 1974 by Leonard Cohen. Used by permission of Stranger Music, Inc. All rights reserved. The line from "The Needle and the Damage Done" by Neil Young (page 63) copyright 1971, Broken Fiddle Music, Inc. Used by permission. All rights reserved. The lines from "Berryman 2" (page 94), from *History*, by Robert Lowell, copyright © 1967, 1968, 1969, 1970, and 1973, by Robert Lowell. Reprinted by permission of Farrar Straus and Giroux, Inc. Excerpt (pages 108–9) from "What lips my lips have kissed, and where, and why" by Edna St. Vincent Millay. From *Collected Poems*, Harper & Row. Copyright © 1923, 1951 by Edna St. Vincent Millay and Norma Millay Ellis. Reprinted by permission. Lines from "Everybody's Talkin' " (page 137) by Fred Neil, copyright 1967 by Third Story Music, Inc. All rights reserved. International copyright secured. Used by permission. The lines from "The Alabama Song," text by Bertolt Brecht (page 150), are from the Kurt Weill/Bertolt Brecht *The Rise and Fall of the City of Mahagonny*, copyright © 1927, Stefan Brecht. Used by permission.

Library of Congress Cataloging-in-Publication Data
Turner, Florence.
  At the Chelsea.
  1. Chelsea Hotel—History. I. Title.
TX941.C44T87   1986   974.7′1   87-8661
ISBN 0-15-109780-1
ISBN 0-15-609310-3 (Harvest/HBJ book : pbk.)

Printed in the United States of America

First United States edition

A B C D E

To Stanley Bard,
Christopher Sinclair-Stevenson, Julian Evans
and all my friends

The people I am most fond of are those who are not quite achieved; who are not very wise, a little mad, 'possessed'. The people 'of sound mind' have little interest for me. The achieved man, the one perfect like an umbrella, does not appeal to me. I am called and doomed, you see, to describe – and what could I say of an umbrella but that it is of no worth on a sunny day? A man slightly possessed is not only more agreeable to me; he is altogether more plausible, more in harmony with the general tune of life, a phenomenon unfathomed yet, and fantastic, which makes it at the same time so confoundedly interesting.

Maxim Gorky

ONE

HOTEL CHELSEA

Dear Florence,

Do you recall that uninhibited night at Hidalgo de Espagne in North Hollywood, when you refused to go on to Puerto Vallarta with Sabu and me? Well, here I am at the Chelsea and I found that you were on the eighth floor. Sabu is dead now and I am staying with Mildred Baker who used also to be in pictures. Anyway, I'm off to Europe tonight to see where it's at. I only know it's not on me. I'll remember that uninhibited night forever, when you refused in North Hollywood to go to Puerto Vallarta.

Your friend from North Hollywood

THUS a letter, anonymous, placed in my box behind the desk of the Chelsea Hotel, 222 West Twenty-Third Street, Manhattan, between Seventh and Eighth Avenues. I never knew who put it there, or why. Whoever it was had *not* stayed with Mildred Baker, a distinguished, long-time resident of the Chelsea who had certainly never 'been in pictures', and the desk clerk had no recollection of the writer or having put the letter in my box.

It does not really matter, since the episode belongs to that realm of the imagination which all of us living at the Chelsea accepted and understood. Each of us had at one time or another refused a mythical invitation to Puerto Vallarta or some other sphere of fantasy. The Chelsea was for us the one place in the world where we could, without fear of criticism, set off on journeys of the mind that were in themselves a joy, whether or not a destination was included. In this sense the hotel has long been a refuge from an unsympathetic world. But those who have left the refuge have also spread its gospel to the world, attracting artists, would-be-artists, followers of the faith from countries everywhere. Not too long ago, Jakov Lind, the Austrian writer, said in an interview, 'You meet people all over the world on this international bohemian circuit, and they'll say, "See you at the Chelsea."'

My own association with the hotel began in 1964, the summer after Kennedy was shot. It had been hotter than ever that year; crime proliferated; and during nights loud with the roar from a million air-conditioners, murder was committed close to the little apartment I had found on York Avenue, not far from the oompah-oompah of the German cafés and restaurants on Eighty-Sixth Street.

The murders had been of two young women and the method of their deaths was especially brutal. Soon afterwards I was robbed, the burglar arriving when I was asleep and walking off with my handbag in which there was $300 saved to attend the MacDowell Colony in New Hampshire where I hoped to write a novel. Detectives arrived. Double murder was still fresh in their minds and I was a relatively young woman.

'Lucky you didn't wake up,' said one.

I borrowed some more money and went off to New Hampshire for a month, but returning to that apartment filled me with dread. It was the nights, of course. A full-time job took care of the days. But busy as I was, it struck me the time had come to move. The problem was where. Apartments within my price range were hard to find. I discussed it with friends, one a painter. We were walking along Twenty-Third Street, eating ice-cream cones, just behind a large Puerto Rican family, also eating. The heat was crucifying; a ship's deep vociferation came to us above the traffic sounds. Three blocks away the Hudson River was bringing a big liner into dock. The sky looked washed out, needing clouds or sunset. We were walking past a wide glass door beneath a striped canopy. The sign above the door read 'CHELSEA HOTEL'.

The painter stopped. Why didn't I try the Chelsea? He knew people who lived there. It was said to be crazy but likeable. We read the brass plaques beside the door, praising past residents: Thomas Wolfe, James T. Farrell, Dylan Thomas, Brendan Behan. Thomas Wolfe! I felt a renewal of youthful awe. Not possible, I decided. The place would be prohibitively expensive. My friends urged me to try.

The desk clerk, a man of Falstaffian girth, informed me that I must speak to the manager, Mr Bard, who was in his office just off the lobby. I left my friends contemplating the eclectic art decorating the walls, and knocked on Mr Bard's door. He was slight and considerably younger than I, seated at a huge desk under a canopy of rosy, somewhat chipped cherubs cavorting on the ceiling above. We talked. Hearing that I had recently been writing a book at the MacDowell Colony, he got happily to his feet. I might have been offering him a gift. He seemed far more interested in this fact than my telling him that I worked as the theatre scout for Metro-Goldwyn-Mayer. Afterwards I was to learn that Stanley, though well endowed with a sense of things material, was genuinely impressed by creativity. His enthusiasm occasionally led him to extremes where he failed to distinguish the real thing from the fake.

Yes, he thought he could accommodate me. To start with, it would only be a small room with the bathroom down the hall. We spoke further of the MacDowell Colony, that richly subsidised collection of the elite set in the woods of New Hampshire. A *New York Times* article once described its function as the care and feeding of artists. Stanley Bard seemed to know all about it. Indeed, another inhabitant of the Chelsea had recently returned from the Colony. Did I know him? Robert Gessner, Professor of Film at New York University. Indeed I knew Bob Gessner. It pleased me to know he would be a neighbour, though he had never mentioned living at the Chelsea. (Later I found out that he too was a newcomer.)

Next evening, I packed up and took a cab downtown. The driver, outspoken in the manner of Manhattan cabbies, asked, 'You really going to live in that dump?'

An explanation of the question soon came. Andy Warhol had just moved in to make his film *Chelsea Girls*. Cabbies and street people alike watched as the tall, spectacularly beautiful transvestites, Candy Darling, Holly Woodlawn, others with equally exaggerated names, strolled through the Chelsea doorway. They were stricken by prurience.

The Chelsea Hotel was built in 1884 by the architectural firm of Hubert, Pirsson and Hoodless, a resounding trio of names. These gentlemen set out to construct the finest co-operative building in New York. Victorian Gothic in design, combined with elements of the Queen Anne or Free Classic style, the Chelsea was built of red brick with wrought-iron balconies across the façade. The apartments were huge, seven rooms or more, and prospective tenants could ask for studios built to personal specification. The ceilings were high, the walls fire-and-sound-proof, and a shallow iron staircase running from the lobby to the roof had a wrought-iron balustrade and mahogany

[3]

banister. Suzanne La Follette, author of the best-seller *Concerning Women* once fell into conversation with an Italian carpenter doing some repairs on the building. He showed her a blueprint of the original Chelsea, and she learned that the floors were laid on cast-iron columns with wrought-iron beams separated by fine, white sand. The walls, indicated the carpenter, were of double brick with air space between.

Every apartment contained one wood-burning fireplace or more, and the flat, red brick roof, designed for strolling and sitting, was set about with clumps of tall chimneys. On the tenth floor, separate, small stairways led to the first penthouses in New York, complete with gardens. These have always been treasured by the residents of the Chelsea and at the time of writing still flourish.

When the Chelsea was built, it was the tallest building in the area. Five years later, in 1889, the Tower Building at 50 Broadway was erected, to be followed by the Flatiron Building at the corner of Fifth Avenue and Twenty-Third Street.

During this period, Twenty-Third Street was the centre of the New York theatre, and it was natural that actors should stay at the Chelsea. Sarah Bernhardt is said to have 'adored' the Chelsea, and always took a suite for the season, bringing her own sheets and a feather-stuffed quilt. She also brought her coffin and, according to her press agent, frequently used it as a bed. She may have been the first to sleep in a coffin at the Chelsea, but she was not the last. Stella Waitzkin, a contemporary artist who sculpts in glass, keeps a made-to-order coffin in her studio, lying in it by way of protest.[1] She doubts that Sarah Bernhardt occupied her coffin for political reasons but there is a kind of satisfaction in knowing two artists had a similar idea. A continuity of aberration.

The elegance of the Chelsea was in keeping with the affluent 'Nineties, the period of the Robber Barons: James ('Jim') Fisk, Jay Gould, Carnegie, Pierpont Morgan and a little later the Vanderbilts and Astors. Twenty-Third Street, as the theatre section of Manhattan, shared the new architectural honours with Twenty-Fourth Street –

---

[1] When the Arab terrorist organization, Black September, invaded the Israeli village during the 1974 Olympic Games, Stella was in Holland with an exhibition of her sculpture. She set up her coffin on trestles outside the gallery and lay down inside, refusing to be moved until the incident ended.

'My art is humanitarian,' she says. 'I must express myself in some dramatic form. My own objection to violence is violence.'

mansion and chateau style, oriental extravagance and Italian baroque. The Opera House Palace competed with the marble halls of Pike's Grand Opera Palace on the corner of Eighth Avenue, soon to be 'one of the widest and most fashionable thoroughfares in the city'.

The twentieth century has no monopoly on violence. The railroad millionaire Fisk, who had started as a peddler from Vermont and lived behind Pike's Grand Opera Palace near the home he had given his mistress, was shot by another of her lovers. And Stanford White, the Frank Lloyd Wright of his day, who had a hide-away on Twenty-Third Street not far from the Chelsea, was murdered too, though perhaps with more cause. He operated a high-class equivalent of today's massage parlours, with drugs, red velvet swings for his girls and pornographic slides; his fate was to be shot by the suffering husband of one of the girls in the red velvet swings.

In the midst of mayhem, the Chelsea's elegance and silence attracted, but the elegance did not endure in the same way the silence has. Remnants of pure Victoriana remain from the time when mahogany prevailed: doors, trim, big corner cupboards, chairs with hand-painted insets, enormous plate-glass mirrors. For the lucky few, some apartments were undamaged by subsequent changes. Indeed, the rooms of the composer Virgil Thomson are still almost the same as when he arrived at the Chelsea in the late 'Thirties.

Many rooms also possessed small, delicate stained-glass windows which either gave on to the dumb-waiter running through the centre of the building from the kitchen, or on to the balconies. The windows which have survived are highly prized by discerning residents, but the dumb-waiter has been boarded up and the Chelsea dining room, one of an original three, is now a studio. In this same dining room, residents ate their evening meals to the music of a trio which sat on a dais next to potted palms.

The second dining room is contained in what became El Quijote's restaurant, an adjunct of the Chelsea and later a touchstone. The conservative Spaniards who ran it struggled over the years to retain their dignity, but little by little, through simple association, reciprocal crime, lust and inter-marriage, they were translated into members of the curious confraternity which made up the inhabitants of the hotel. Such was its influence.

The third of the dining rooms has been chopped into the areas that make up the front desk, a storage room and the space reserved for public telephones. There is no elegance here, save perhaps the marble floor.

The original kitchen is still used by the Spanish chefs – in my time the head chef was José. Designed to be completely self-contained, the Chelsea once baked its own bread, stocked its own big wine-cellar and in the basement prepared fresh fish and meat on solid wooden tables. Cooking smells still waft through the big chimneys onto the roof, smells that have changed over the years from French to Greek to Spanish.

By 1905 tremendous changes (for the worse) were taking place at the Chelsea. The co-operative was sold and turned into an hotel, the theatre district moved uptown to Broadway. Next to a shabby parking lot on the opposite side of Twenty-Third Street from the Chelsea, there is a name in bronze sunk into the pavement, PROCTOR, commemorating a theatre that once seated 2800. Opened in 1889 by F.F. Proctor, a former acrobat, its policy was to put on continuous daily vaudeville, and many of the artists appearing there stayed at the Chelsea: Lillie Langtry, 'Jersey Lily'; Lillian Russell; Eva Tanguay, simultaneously vulgar and wistful and often clad in a costume made entirely of bright mirrors. Harry Lauder was a favourite at Proctor's, as were Lottie Collins and Vesta Victoria the Cockney star, and France's Yvette Guilbert. Today, all that remains of the Proctor Theatre is the name on the pavement from which the letter 'T' is missing.

Despite these changes, the Chelsea remained a home for artists in a furiously competitive world. Mark Twain took up residence. O. Henry, who always registered under a different name, lived somewhat drunkenly on the fourth floor. Hart Crane and Sherwood Anderson moved in and the 'Ash Can' school of painting was represented by John Sloan and others.

The Depression arrived. Fifty years on, Alice Tibbetts, youthful-looking and delicately made, recalled what happened to the Chelsea between the wars. An Irish family, the Knotts, took over, using the entire second floor as their offices. Alice is sure they got together one day and said, 'Let's go uptown and buy that Chelsea.' The results were shocking. The Knotts were to devastate the building and wreak havoc on the Chelsea's beauty. They smashed huge plate-glass mirrors, chopped up suites in order to make more room for transients, and ruined the ground floor by putting in a ceiling where before it had been possible to look straight up the stairwell to the roof. The appealing symmetry of the cast-iron balconies was left untouched but following

[6]

this architectural surgery there appeared, inevitably, dilapidation and neglect. Nothing was done to keep the building in repair and, like my taxi driver, people in the neighbourhood regarded the Chelsea as a slum filled with dubious characters. In the meantime those who lived there did their best to ignore the new owners and get on with their lives, each according to his bent. Alice Tibbetts lived near the poet Edgar Lee Masters. Theirs was a legendary, very close friendship, lasting until his death in 1950. Afterwards, she continued living at the Chelsea and speaks of those vivid poverty-stricken, creative times with love. No one had money, but if a story or book or painting managed to sell, there would be enough for 'a little old party', or to go dancing in white gloves with Edgar at the St Regis Hotel. But mostly the writers and painters relaxed at home among themselves. Alice often invited people for simple meals, and a favourite among the regular visitors was Robert Flaherty, father of the documentary film and, in Alice's words, 'a darling man'. Flaherty was enchanted by the Chelsea. *Louisiana Story* began there and Virgil Thomson wrote the music in his studio on the ninth floor.

Thomas Wolfe was another favourite of Alice's and Masters's, though he 'had terrible tantrums'. Gargantuan in all ways, he was apt to pick fights when drunk, which was often. But he too loved the Chelsea and had planned to make his next book about it just before he died. He, like Alice, felt the hotel to be a happy place and a sanctuary. He lived and wrote *You Can't Go Home Again* in Room 831. It was my own room for eleven years, but I remember it rather differently from the description which appeared in Harper's in 1937:

> I shall never forget my first visit to Tom at the Chelsea. He had a three-room suite which sounds more magnificent than it was, for the rooms were dark and dingy. But they had the advantage of ceilings high enough so that he ran no risk of bumping his head. The most impressive feature of the suite was the bathroom, which was quite large with a toilet set on a raised platform. Tom called it 'the Throne Room'. By the first of February, 1936, Wolfe had launched into his intensive work on his book. His cratefuls of mss. were all unpacked and scattered around his three big, high-ceilinged rooms at the old Chelsea.

It is likely the Knott family cut up Wolfe's 'suite'. In my time, there was only one large room with a space-saving 'Murphy' kitchen built into one corner. The bathroom was indeed a step up from the room, but contained not only the w.c. but a pink porcelain bath that could never have accommodated Wolfe's bulk. I was fond of imagining him working in those surroundings, pretending that his memory inspired me. Possibly it did. Whatever the truth, there was pride in living in that room with its uneven view of the Hudson, where I could see big liners and freighters and, finally, vast tankers moving up the river, bisected in the latter years by a huge building on the water-front so that one saw them only fore and aft, eviscerated for a brief time by wanton architecture. Sunsets too. All this Wolfe must have seen.

In *The Web and the Rock*, Wolfe wrote, autobiographically, 'He ate and drank the city to its roots – and through all that spring not once did it occur to him that he had left not even a heelprint on its stony pavements?' Elsewhere, he wrote the description that could apply to many inhabitants of the Chelsea: '. . . he wants to be the greatest poet, the greatest writer, the greatest composer, or the greatest leader in the world – and he wants to paint instead of own the greatest painting in the world.' Few achieved what Wolfe achieved, even though they lived longer than he. But the will was there, and the obsession.[1]

Theodore Dreiser often came to visit at the Chelsea, or gave return parties at his place in Washington Square. His ugliness was striking, but, Alice says, one soon forgot it, watching him 'sitting there folding and unfolding his handkerchief' before joining in the conversation or listening with amusement as Edgar Lee Masters made up stories which John Cowper Powys, the Welsh writer who then lived in the Village, said were Chaucerian.

It seems to have been a specially fruitful time for artists. Writers may have prevailed, among them Suzanne La Follette, whom Edgar Lee Masters called 'our blue stocking'. But there were others. Across from Room 1010, where Edgar Lee Masters lived near Alice, was Edward C. Caswell, 'a wonderful neighbour. He would go out and buy some Chinese food and I would make coffee and thus we eked out a meagre evening meal. Poor though we all were, there was no pervading gloom. We could afford only cheap sherry in large jugs and sometimes rye with water – but it was enough. And there were endless pots of coffee.

[1] In the 'Seventies a writer named Dan Mason adapted 'Look Homeward Angel' for the theatre and the play was subsequently performed at the Gate Theatre, Dublin. Dan kept a man-sized plaster statue of an angel in his room.

'Mr Caswell,' said Alice, 'regularly made the drawings for the front page of the *Villager* – there are priceless views of lovely doorways, and so on. But when he became ill and had to be taken to hospital the story is that the management simply swept hundreds of those wondrous things into the hall and out . . . Caswell sat in the hospital, where I saw him last, suffering over what would become of his drawings. I hope he never knew.'

John Sloan and his wife Dolly had what was then the only duplex apartment on the tenth and eleventh floors. In the studio at the top of their stairs were stacks of paintings. Sloan was teaching at the time at the Student Art League and bringing in a small income, but Dolly, alas, drank too much. A tiny woman and Irish, she was a fighter, having been one of the early strikers in Philadelphia when there was a shirtwaist-makers' strike. Alice Tibbetts still has an etching of John Sloan and herself, seated on a rock, given to her by Dolly and signed, 'Always poor, but together'.

In the 1920s and '30s, Frank Wren, another painter, had a small permanent gallery of his work in the lobby. This was a curious right he enjoyed by virtue of having been born in the hotel and the fact that his father, Frank Sr, had been a founding member of the co-operative when original stock was issued to the tenants.[1] Wren also became a dealer, handling outstanding American painters like John Birchfield and Edward Hopper. A lawyer, born in 1869 in Kansas, Edgar Lee Masters moved to Chicago, writing poetry and practising law at the same time. His best-selling book of poetry was, of course, *Spoon River Anthology*, but Alice feels there is much too much emphasis on it and that all his later poetry suffered as a result of its success, critics saying (as critics will), 'It isn't *Spoon River*.' Some imagined he never wrote anything else, though from 1902 to the time when he moved to the Chelsea Hotel in 1930, he wrote forty books and a play, *Maximillian*. And during his twelve years at the Chelsea, he wrote eighteen more books, priding himself for having experimented in more varieties of verse than any other American poet.

'He loved humour,' Alice recalls, adding that one of his favourite pastimes was exchanging comic rhymes with H.L. Mencken and Theodore Dreiser. But, like Dreiser's, his work was controversial, and Alice feels his lack of recognition was due to Victorian America.

For Masters, who had left his wife and family, Alice was 'Anita', the

[1] A portrait of Frank Wren the elder still hangs behind the front desk.

[9]

woman addressed in his long poem 'The Hotel Chelsea' in which he incorrectly forecast its demolition, though correctly, and sadly, forecasting that 'Anita' will long outlive him:

Anita! Soon this Chelsea Hotel
Will vanish before the city's merchant greed,
Wreckers will wreck it, and in its stead
More lofty walls will swell

This old street's populace. Then who will know
About its ancient grandeur, marble stairs,
Its paintings, onyx-mantels, courts, the heirs
Of a time now long ago?

Who will then know that Mark Twain used to stroll
In the gorgeous dining-room, that princesses,
Poets and celebrated actresses
Lived here and made its soul;

In after years, so often made and unmade
By the changing generations, until today
It stands a tomb of happiness passed away,
Of an era long overlaid?

What loves were lived here, what despairs endured,
What children born here, and what mourners went
Out of its doors, what peace and what lament
These rooms knew, long obscured

Will be more lost when fifty years from hence
The place thereof will have no memory,
When men must hunt its picture, so to see
What it looked like amid this turbulence!

Few now remember even the noted names
That loved its hospitality in past years.
Who will remember me when wrecking shears
Clip like a leaf this room of troubled aims,

And make this window one with the sky's space,
By which I sat looking into the court?
This table that I write on will not report
My dreams, gone by without a trace.

[10]

There will not be a seat for any ghost,
No room left for a musing ghost to smile
On kisses, vows, regrets, that for a while
Made life, and then were lost.

The blue-eyed woman who went out and in
The entrance door, time and the tooth thereof
Will take her, take the man who gave her love,
Both will be lost ere twenty years begin.

With purest love this woman was beloved;
With pain her lover looked upon her grief,
Her past, and strove to give her heart relief,
Himself by Life so moved.

All this will be but currents of the air
Veering and lost. Tell me how souls can be
Such flames of suffering and of ecstasy,
Then fare as the winds fare?

Tell me how love that fills the human heart
With a sense of things eternal must submit
To what is eyeless, and is infinite,
And hears so soon the word 'depart?'

Anita! You can perpetuate by thought
What we have lived, when this hotel is gone.
Passing its site remember I was one
Who sought for peace and found it not.

Remember that I loved you, scarce could bear
My helplessness to give your spirit thrift —
Remember this as with the tide you drift,
Others will not remember, nor even care.

There was some bitterness in Alice's voice when in later years she talked of the management's failure to include her friend's name on the brass plaque beside the entrance. However, recognition came from another direction on the day after my return to the Chelsea for a visit, in September 1984. Talking to a friend in the lobby, I saw Alice emerging from the elevator with a tall, grey-haired man. She introduced me. It was Signor Chiti from Milan, a passionate reader of

Edgar Lee Masters and with the largest collection of his works in the world. He had come all the way from Italy to meet Alice and see the hotel where Masters lived.

I watched them leave for lunch somewhere, Alice smartly dressed and pretty, looking for all the world as though, once more, she might be on her way in white gloves to go dancing with her beloved at the St Regis Hotel. 'Anita' in love.

In 1940 David Bard, a Hungarian, bought the Chelsea from the Knott family allegedly for $50,000. His partners were a flinty, muscular man named Krauss, and plump little Mr Gross. Bard's son Stanley, a schoolboy, was often in the hotel, learning to operate the elevators with the help of a black bellman named Purnell Kennedy.

It was now time, according to David's son Stanley thirty years later, that 'the slow process of rebuilding and revitalizing began', although his is not a view shared by Suzanne La Follette, who recalls that 'what I saw happening to this building was tragic'.

Krauss, expressionless and tough, continued to wreck the building, apparently having no interest in its intrinsic beauty, breaking more of the big mirrors and building more partitions, so that big rooms were reduced to little ones with papery walls through which occupants could hear one another. However, those with leases refused to move and large pockets of rooms managed to preserve their original calm.

During the Second World War, David Bard joined forces with the Church World Service and Catholic Committees, placing European refugees in the hotel, crowding families into spaces meant only for one or two people. A few residents like Alice Tibbetts remained – as did Virgil Thomson.

The composer came to the Chelsea from Paris 'in 1937 or 1938', he cannot be quite certain, and took up quarters on the ninth floor behind original Chelsea double doors. He still has three rooms, including his kitchen and bath. The original built-in mahogany furnishings could produce a brooding atmosphere, but the paraphernalia of work in progress, the tributes to his brilliance, the products of a composer's life nullify this. So does humour. In the bathroom is a row of Delft blue tiles where a nude maiden frolics in turn with a porpoise, a lobster, a whale. There is an apricot-coloured love-seat, a big velvet couch, books, scores in piles on the table and a grand piano. In another room, a long work table holds more scores. There is a sense of purpose and of fun about the rooms. Virgil wrote a lot of music at the Chelsea – still

[12]

writes it – though one of his most famous works, *Four Saints in Three Acts*, (written together with Gertrude Stein) was composed in Paris. At one time Virgil and his friends John Houseman and Orson Welles wrote for the Negro Theatre in Harlem. He wrote music for a black *Macbeth* in which Canada Lee played Banquo. Canada Lee was also a boxer and trained one of the Chelsea's favourite black bellmen, Charles Beard, as a welter-weight.

When he became music critic for the *Herald Tribune*, Virgil invited one of the black actors from *Four Saints in Three Acts* to help him. The work was piling up and he needed an amanuensis. Considered in the light of today's integration at the Chelsea, it is astounding to note that, in Virgil's words, 'since the Chelsea Hotel did not at that time house coloured lodgers', Leonard Franklin, a tenor soloist whom Virgil called Saint, had to find an apartment nearby and walk to work every day.

One day I met Virgil in the lobby. He was carrying his dirty laundry in a bag; I held a fat book, a life of Edith Piaf by her sister. Virgil gave it a glance and said, 'She lived in the house, you know.'

The house. Yes, it was a house and a home. I found out later that Virgil had saved Piaf from disaster after other critics in New York blasted her performance. Virgil was indignant and, as music critic of the *Herald Tribune*, took them to task, pointing out that they had not bothered to understand the singer's special idiom. It seemed natural after that for Piaf to move into the Chelsea.

Virgil continues to live and work at the Chelsea and his works continue to be performed. A few years ago, in 1985, his opera about Byron was produced at Lincoln Center. There is a sustained buoyancy about him and an air of perky wisdom, though the years have mounted up. But he was one of the great music critics of the century as well as a liberal, and it is as well to recall his ability to annihilate the second- and third-rate and guard one's words. Fittingly, one of Virgil's close good friends at the Chelsea was the writer Mary McCarthy, who is also equipped with a quick and searing mind, and an enormous impatience with mediocrity.

In the 'Forties the Chelsea reflected, as it has always reflected, the disorganized life on the outside. Refugees from Europe had made their mark and the halls must have been dingy with latent fear, humiliation and a sense of over-crowding. But there were artists among them, and several stayed on to make the Chelsea their home.

[13]

With the 'Fifties, new artists arrived to delight, confound and ultimately irritate those already in residence. Among them was Dylan Thomas, continuing the alcoholic precedent begun by Thomas Wolfe. He died of alcoholism in St Vincent's Hospital a few blocks away: St Vincent's which, over the years, was for many of us a home from home.

Ten years later, Brendan Behan rowdily arrived with his young friend Peter Arthur. They had just been thrown out of the Bristol Hotel on West Forty-Eighth where they made nightly spectacles of themselves, although Peter's job was to sober up his companion. It was his jaunty but hollow claim that he was the only one who could. Peter, a young Irish seaman from Dundalk — 'the Dodge City of Ireland', as he called it, and the heart of the IRA — fell in with Behan in California. They travelled around together and then separated, Peter returning to sea after appearing in *The Quare Fellow* in Dublin. He was anchored off Petty's Island (in New Jersey) when he received word at his ship that Behan was in the midst of a major crisis. Thus their reunion at the Bristol Hotel.

They moved into the Chelsea, possibly guided there by Behan's publisher, Bernard Geis, who had given him an introduction to Katherine Dunham, black dancer and anthropologist. It was she, Peter and, on occasion, the composer George Kleinsinger, who became Behan's baby-sitters. He managed to write *Brendan Behan's New York* and *Confessions of a Rebel* between alcoholic bouts and Peter stayed by him faithfully, denying that he led Behan astray. Indeed, to Peter it was the reverse. 'Brendan Behan deliberately made me an alcoholic,' he told me, not without some satisfaction.

Behan continued his loud, disorderly existence at the Chelsea. He shouted obscenities down the stairwell, chased the maids and went drinking with George Kleinsinger until all alcohol was forbidden him, and his minders permitted him only five dollars a day pocket money. George composed a 'Lament and Jig' for Behan in which the latter joined in full tongue, introducing an Irish folk song. He liked to sing in George's studio, but here George's pet birds flew freely and sang their own songs. Behan found them irritating. 'Stop the fucking competition!' he would shout. Frustrated once, he stole twenty dollars from Peter Arthur's wallet and when Peter complained said, 'Go along with it; we're having fun.'

Peter, who had the face of a battered angel, stayed on at the Chelsea after Behan's departure and subsequent death in Dublin. After all,

[14]

merchant seamen had been staying there for fifty years. The hotel fascinated him. He wanted desperately to identify with it and was humiliated by what he considered his lack of creativity, unaware that his great gift of storytelling placed him well within the category of artist. He also had to come to terms with his Irish Catholicism. The life-style of most of the Chelsea's residents offended his sense of morality, which prevailed strangely despite his own wild way of living. But gradually the Chelsea cured him of hypocrisy, showing him, he told me, 'a whole new way of life'. He met Arthur Miller, the playwright, and started reading 'for the first time in my life'. He even attended poetry readings and 'discovered little talents I never even knew I possessed, and people whose professions I'd never even heard of'.

Peter and I became good friends and had long conversations, during which he asked me questions mainly to do with writing. I told him what a thesaurus was, and marvelled when he told me that, while admitting frankly to his bisexuality, he had no idea what the word pornography meant until it was explained to him. Inspired to learn and to go on living in the Chelsea, he nevertheless had to leave from time to time to earn money. This he did as a tank-cleaner, a dangerous occupation. But he went back to sea and stuck with the job until a bad accident put him into hospital. Here he had time to think, and knew his secret ambition was to be a writer, although many of the stories that circulated in his life were not stories that he told, but stories about him. He was accused of informing to narcotic agents, which was untrue. He was referred to as a pimp, supplying a demand whenever there was one; this, he said candidly, was true. But none of it mattered after the day arrived when he was referred to as an intellectual. 'This,' he admitted with satisfaction, 'was my biggest kick.'

One thing Peter feared in himself was his violence, which was kept under control, or not in evidence at all, until he started drinking. At the hotel he was asked by the management to act as a kind of security guard wherever undesirables such as junkies − to qualify, these were transient junkies, not the kind in residence − or leather boys infiltrated. He could not fully acquiesce to this, conscious of his suppressed Irish fury and the awareness that on occasions he might be risking his life, for nothing. So he departed again, telling me it was because Stanley Bard, the manager, was putting too much pressure on him. He left a debt as well. It was not because he could not pay it. He had received generous compensation as a result of his accident. He left because of a curious streak of stubborn Irish pride. 'I will not pay you because you used me,' he told the manager. 'And anyone who uses me, pays me.' It didn't really make sense. And in any case, Peter never really left the Chelsea. He returned and still returns off and on. No longer a drinking man, his temperament shows its natural good humour and wit and he can still tell a story better than anyone in the Chelsea. In one way Peter belonged at the Chelsea from the start. For years the hotel had accommodated apprentice British seamen and those who had retired. They kept their own rhythm, observing and never commenting. I liked talking with them; it made a change. One, elderly, and with a sea-worthy face and an Irish accent, told me about Roger Casement.

'He stopped at the Chelsea, collecting for Fianna Fail.' And he wrote it down for me in green ink.

I chose to believe him.

Roosevelt's 'New Deal' had made its way into the Chelsea in the person of Harry Hopkins, the gifted American administrator who charted the federal relief programme in the Depression and also ran the Works Progress Administration (WPA) which benefited large numbers of writers and painters during the slump. Another resident who became his co-administrator was Jake Baker, a mining engineer from Colorado and a distinguished publisher, founder of the Vanguard Press which published some of the most brilliant radical writing of the day: Jack London on socialism; Leo Tolstoy's work on pacificism; Upton Sinclair's *The Jungle*; Thorstein Veblen's classic study *The Theory of the Leisure Class*; and *The Letters of Sacco and Vanzetti*. Jake Baker was outstanding in that his books did not make a profit, largely because of his ambition to provide a young readership with the opportunity to read great and stimulating writers. Vanguard Press had been sold in the late 'Twenties to James Henle, a former New York World reporter, but Jake was still at the Chelsea when I arrived and we became great friends. He called me his 'cousin from over the mountain', having known my father, Bryant Turner, whose ranch, the Trinchera – where I grew up – lay over a 14,000-foot peak, Mount Blanca, from Jake's own ranch.

Jake's wife Mildred has always been interested in painting and sculpture, and still sits on committees of various museums in New York and New Jersey. She is elegant, forthright and beautiful and at

[16]

one time drove a Silver Cloud Rolls-Royce which delighted me, though Mildred dislikes its memory. To me the juxtaposition of a stately Rolls and the Chelsea Hotel is no less rewarding an image than Virgil Thomson carrying his dirty laundry through the Chelsea lobby watched indifferently by black pimps hung about with gold chains in plantation hats, jump-suits of startling hue and high-heeled gold boots. The pimps were not, as the Chelsea's reputation would have it, a fixture, but appeared from time to time and were allowed to stay when tenants fell in arrears with rent. Stanley Bard charged them twice as much to make up the difference, and, seeing them arrive, we who were in debt would sigh with relief, knowing we were safe for a few more weeks. The pimps, unknowingly, were patrons of the arts.

In the 'Fifties, which people sometimes associate only with Dylan Thomas and Brendan Behan, other outstanding artists arrived. One early arrival was the novelist James T. Farrell. Like me, he desperately needed a place to live and work and moved into the hotel without prior knowledge, delighted when he found out that his old friends Jake Baker and Suzanne La Follette were also residents. Farrell renewed his friendship with others: Edgar Lee Masters, John Sloan, and several writers he had known before. He thought of them all as belonging to a 'once vigorously alive cultural and political American environment from which many of us breathed knowledge and inspiration, ideals and purpose'.

Farrell's residence coincided with the flood of Hungarian refugees who wandered confusedly through the lobby, furnished then, with its heavy chairs and marble-topped tables, in what Charles James the great couturier later called sub-Ruskin or Austrian Bordello. Farrell made two lengthy visits to the Chelsea, the first in the 'Fifties and the second in the early 'Sixties, when he was dumbfounded to find his name on a brass obituary plaque beside the entrance, along with Arthur B. Davies, Robert Flaherty, O. Henry, Dylan Thomas, Brendan Behan, Thomas Wolfe. Farrell and Jake Baker, greatly amused, speculated as to the form of his demise: unnatural causes or suicide? Farrell sat down and wrote a poem entitled 'Obituary'.

> One James T. (for Thomas) Farrell
> Who might have been this
> And who might have been that,

But who might have been
Neither this nor that,
And who wrote too much,
And who kissed too much
For all of his friends
(He needed no enemies)
That man J.T.F.
Died last night
Of a deprivation of time.
He willed his dust
To the public domain.

Talking to a would-be writer in the Chelsea lobby one night, Farrell said it had been impossible for him to hold down a job and write as well. So he had made an 'all or nothing' decision. He became famous and was nominated by Adlai Stevenson for the Nobel Prize just at the time when he was fighting an eviction for non-payment of rent. (He does not say if this happened at the Chelsea. I feel it is unlikely, for Stanley would certainly have brought in the pimps.) Soon afterwards, President Kennedy invited him to the White House for dinner and he was forced to borrow money for the fare to Washington. On his return to New York, he found a cheque for $1100 waiting from an Italian publisher.

I particularly like this story. It illustrates so comfortingly the eternal possibilities on which artists live most of the time. The possibilities of success; the near-miss followed by a sudden unexpected hit; hope. Hope mitigating the desperate disappointment of an editor's rejection, of a failed audition, of a gallery's refusal. Hope mitigating fear. I wish I had met Farrell, but he was just before my time. Did that generation abhor materialism? Certainly it seemed to take more chances: Farrell without funds in what should have been a moment of triumph; Thomas Wolfe filling boxes with manuscripts and having the luck to find an editor like Maxwell Perkins. This is no doubt romanticizing. Artists always want money, but on their own terms. One has to eat, but the need for recognition is the most important aspect of creativity. I knew one writer at the Chelsea who wrote dozens of pulp novels a year under different names for a flat sum. The trouble was that he found he was unable to turn back to his own ideas, and that he had reached the point, too, of finding excellence where there was none. When I confessed myself unable to summon up enthusiasm for one of his works, he was furious with me, though I detected the source of his fury in his own secret knowledge.

Instant success and acclaim may possibly be every artist's dream, and one that few achieve and more spend a life-time waiting for. However, one long-term resident, Ben Burman, who wrote books about the Mississippi, might have found it worth the wait when he sold *Steamboat Round The Bend* to Walt Disney for around one million dollars not long ago, when he was in his eighties. Despite thirty years of Chelsea living, he and his wife, Alice Caddy, a painter, promptly moved out.

Arthur Miller, another long-term resident, also departed – although not for the same reasons. His wife did not want to raise their child in the Chelsea atmosphere. But although long-term dwellers like Ben Burman and Arthur Miller left, others such as Mildred Baker and Virgil Thomson remained and still are there. Jake Baker died in the early 'Sixties, but Mildred moved into a smaller apartment and is unlikely ever to live anywhere else. As to the less affluent or successful, we were forced to move out because we were unable to pay the rent, despite the ad hoc social security arrangements provided by bringing in the pimps. Sometimes when the more successful moved, they returned, unable to endure or work in the world outside. A film-maker I knew called Shirley Clarke is one of these. After years at the Chelsea, she moved to California, but returned in 1983 to take a lease and work in peace and comfort.

What is it about the Chelsea that makes it so appealing, so important to artists and would-be artists? Perhaps they generate their own atmosphere, one composed of self-reliance, self-adulation, self-confidence that would all be dissipated in the atmosphere of orthodox living. James Farrell summed it up: 'Marcel Proust devotes a long section of his great work to "Place Names". Proust discusses place names in France. In America there is less richness of place names and the places of place names. The Hotel Chelsea is a landmark, qualifies as a place name – thereby a place. And for me personally, the Hotel Chelsea is a private place name in my memory.'

In general the Chelsea has always represented or reflected what goes on in the world without. There was the elegance of the 'Nineties; the Great War; the Depression and World War Two with its aftermath of refugees. The 'Fifties displayed fewer social transitions, but

[19]

Dr Robert Oppenheimer took up residence; later Peter Brook leased a large apartment; Arthur C. Clarke maintained a suite where he stayed whenever he visited the United States from Sri Lanka.

Yet for the world without, for the street people and taxi drivers, the building had been a dump from the beginning of the century, and still was. It became even more so in their eyes with the arrival of the psychedelic age and rock music.

It was at this point that I moved into the Chelsea.

TWO

MOVING IN

MY arrival was unattended save by the taxi driver who, as I remember, did not bother to help me with my luggage. But a small, very dark 'Nigra' – as he called himself sometimes – named Percy took charge and after brief conversation at the desk, we ascended in the hand-operated elevator to the fourth floor. The corridors were shadowed; the walls a kind of dirty beige. But I heard singing and responded with pleasure to Percy's kind efficiency. I'd like it here, he assured me, and I wasn't to give any mind to those who spoke 'sourcastically' (it was the first of many malapropisms I was to hear) about the place. He twinkled in his green uniform like a dark gnome. There was, of course, the suspicious awareness in his eyes common to all bellmen in all city hotels. Nevertheless, I trusted him and thanked him for making sure I had a clean towel. Money changed hands. This seemed to surprise him. Chelsea residents did not tip as a rule. But as stated I was fully employed at the time, being theatre scout for Metro-Goldwyn-Mayer. This was a nine-to-five job, so to speak, though my clock was far more elastic since I was required to see every new play in and around New York – Philadelphia, New Haven, Washington DC – and as a result of getting to bed in the small hours, had the privilege of going to work late.

I was to find that the job did not impress my new friends in the Chelsea. People who had regular jobs were regarded as belonging to the Establishment even though in my case there was something vaguely creative in the work. Shirley Clarke, for instance, looked on films made by MGM as a little ludicrous, but at the same time hoping the big money would find a way into her hands so she could get on with the brilliant underground movies she made and is still making.

I held no specious view about Metro-Goldwyn-Mayer, never seeing myself as the executive I actually was. My salary, accepted out of ignorance, since I had come from London where I had been paid far less, seemed to me a massive sum. I soon found out it was not. I earned, I found out, less than did a private secretary. Less than my boss's

[21]

secretary, or the receptionists who manned the front desks. But looking back, it strikes me that this unworldliness made it possible for me to accept the Chelsea and everything about it. I belonged there far more than in the world of big movie-making business. Still, I was pretty good at my job and there were perks like first-class air fare and two aisle seats in the third row for try-outs and first nights. I always invited a poverty-stricken friend to use the second seat if the play was in New York. And the salary, mean as it was — $8500 a year — enabled me to move from my dark little room on the fourth floor to Thomas Wolfe's old apartment on the eighth. This cost $200 a month and became my home for the next ten and a half years.

The elder Mr Bard, who had originally bought the hotel from the Knott family, died the year I moved in, 1964, and his son Stanley took over. Behind the desk were Mr Zolt, a gentle opera enthusiast, and Mr Applebaum, a handsome man who was always immaculate in four-in-hand and grey suiting. Although Mr Zolt accepted every situation with equanimity, 'Apple', as he was often known, often reacted angrily, shouting at guests with problems. Both of them were Hungarian refugees with a limited knowledge of English, and both wore out quickly and died during my first year at the Chelsea.

When Stanley took over, it was Gross, the second partner, and Apple who taught him to be a hotelier. Krauss, the third partner, regarded most people, and certainly the residents, as cretins to be endured. He was utterly devoid of aesthetic taste, or any taste. One day I watched him, in one of his appalling efforts at re-decoration, demolish a huge plate-glass mirror in one of the corridors, smashing the beautiful glass with furious wielding of his axe, still unsmiling but giving off emanations of mindless pleasure. It was a nasty sight. Krauss, nevertheless, seemed popular with the rest of the staff, possibly because he willingly performed — without much success — dirty jobs like fixing the plumbing or hunting for rats in the vast reaches of the Chelsea cellar.

Stanley turned over the job of secretary to Eve Tabor, a hugely efficient woman drawn to the arts — she said — and became full-time manager. His influence was disturbing to some of the older residents who had known his father. They wondered, as others came to wonder, if he considered the hotel's real value and its sense of history, or whether or not he actually understood the quality of his tenants. In the long run, was it not perhaps the quick turnover with profits that interested him most? 'If Stanley's heart was of gold he'd sell it,' one of the black maids said to me once.

These were hard words and have been disproved, since his heart, while possibly a trifle alloyed, is still there, and his understanding of the hotel has been forced upon him by the people living under its roof. Being young himself at the time he took over, he was tolerant of the young and understood very well the new vernacular and way of dress which so disturbed Apple. He himself remained in appearance middle class with a swing, although in time long association with the artists rubbed off on him, and in his way, he is unique. Where else in the world was there a hotel manager allowing bills to soar, and himself to be bullied by the guilty delinquents because he believed somehow that the delinquent at some future date would pay off as an artist? Yet Stanley too was capable of bullying, and not always in private.

Delinquents would slink through the lobby hoping not to be observed and be called into his jumbled office like schoolchildren to the headmaster's study. There, surrounded by filing cabinets and staring up at the gleeful cherubs, residents in debt listened as Stanley asked them to pay up. When of necessity people were locked out of their rooms, there were screeching scenes below the cherubs. Even a stronger man than Stanley, or one unused to temperamental people, would have been shaken. But he was, after all, in the position of baby-sitter for several hundred people: artists and those who for some reason of their own like to be near artists, or perhaps willy-nilly find themselves in juxtaposition to the breed.

Stanley's great interest has always been painting; he often took an artist's latest work in lieu of rent. Over the years he has no doubt amassed quite a collection, for he took home those paintings he preferred. The others were left on display in the lobby, some of great intrinsic worth, others of no worth whatsoever. At the time of my arrival, the lobby walls were thickly hung with offerings, a kind of fine arts gallery exclusive to the Chelsea. Some were dreadful; others superb. Over the doorway was a long painting, 'Grey Nude', by an Indian named Paramsee. Eugenie Gershoy's delightful sculpture in papier mâché, 'Puppets of Artists', distinguished the big window left of the entrance. René Shapshak's frieze in plaster, Seven Arts, hung over the original nineteenth-century fireplace. There were paintings by Larry Rivers, André Francois, Dartel, Sidney Cross (another Sidney – Nolan – although a resident did not choose to exhibit, or probably did

[23]

not have to); a quite execrable and very large painting of tulips in primary colours by one Jan Cremer, a young Dutchman who could not decide whether he was a painter, a poet or just an all-round genius (he was none of these things); several mobiles of steel, of green neon, of glass – this last by Kocise, an Argentinian. Allan Jacquet's large silkscreen hung in one corner and in another Lynne Hultberg's multi-colour abstract.

Many of these paintings are still there, including the Larry Rivers, but one by Jackson Pollock has disappeared – possibly removed to Stanley's house – and I am pleased to say Jan Cremer's rigid rows of tulips have also vanished. Over the years, from time to time, new paintings appear.

One laments the disappearance of the Willem de Kooning, John Hultberg, Brett Whiteley (an Australian with a Harpo Marx explosion of hair). Sculptors at the Chelsea seem over the years to have fared better than painters and certainly better than writers, who could never get away with presenting Stanley with a manuscript as a substitute for rent. Curious, that. A book has to be proven, printed and bound before it can be passed as potential currency, whereas the mere fact of paint and canvas that can be hung and looked at seems to evoke security. Who would have accepted on spec a box-full of Thomas Wolfe's ramblings? Just a lot of paper. Writers are second-class citizens until proven in the market-place. Can it be that this is why they are constantly subjected to humiliating comments from non-writers who seem to think they are just as capable of writing a book as the next person? That the manipulation and understanding of words is anyone's perogative? The irony is that Sunday painters abound, certainly ever since Winston Churchill.

The Warhol era, just under way when I arrived, would have pleased Julian Eltinge, the famous female impersonator of the 'Nineties who had stayed at the Chelsea. But what would he have made of Patti Cakes or Cherry Vanilla, who blew in with the days of Pop Art and Happenings? They wore see-through blouses and lurex hot pants and painted their faces in a manner that must have been the forerunner of today's facial decorations. Patti liked giving her friends a special brand of vaginal ticklers in different flavours. She was absurd, corrupt and ridiculously innocent.

My colleagues at MGM showed great curiosity about the Chelsea, while at the same time deriding it as a nest of weirdos, the assumption being that we were all tinged with Warhol-style bizarreness. The world of big business and the Chelsea were far apart; I could never bridge the gap. My new friends, as I gradually met them, looked on MGM as an evil necessity, labelling themselves, perhaps rightly, as elitist. For a year or two, it seemed I would have to take sides. Working for the most powerful movie company in the world, at the same time I knew my sympathies were with the Chelsea artists.

Few of the residents were about when I went out to work, but there were early risers who soon became familiar to me. There was a tall, nervous man around forty years old who never went out of the front door without pausing to stare fixedly at himself in the big mirror remaining on one wall. But he only used one eye, the right, pushing his face against the wall so that the left eye saw nothing. This strange communion with – was it his better half? – lasted only a couple of minutes before he straightened up and departed for his destination. The desk clerk was non-committal and I never found out his name. Then there was the Woman Who Talked to God. Sometimes she rode down in the elevator with me. Not long after my arrival, one of the elevators became automated. This did not mean it was reliable. It stuttered and stopped, sometimes between floors, and generated fear and uncertainty in all of us. At first I thought the Woman Who Talked to God did so for a specific reason, perhaps praying, 'Please God, let us make it to the ground floor.' Later I found out that she was addressing Him for reasons of her own: middle-aged and nondescript, save for her undoubted friendship with the Almighty, she had no interest in what went on around her. She moved in her own aura. We stood aside to let her out first, and might just have been shadows on the perimeter of her consciousness. But one morning the Woman Who Talked to God astounded me by turning her attention my way. 'When God speaks,' she said coldly, 'the restaurants close.' Not long after this, she was evicted. Not even God could help her with her rent and there was a flurry of police and ambulance men before she vanished from our midst. I missed her.

Elderly twins, perhaps they were only sisters, took her place in the elevator when I left for work. They dressed identically in green or pink with dazzling sequins and high-heeled shoes. They smiled carefully, fearful perhaps of cracking what appeared to be skilfully coloured enamel on their faces. I imagined them to be a song-and-dance act left over from days gone by.

[25]

The elevators were a leitmotif of our existence. Purnell the black bellman, who had been longer at the hotel than any of the other staff, hand-operated the elevator which was left of the desk as one entered. This, being more or less to be counted on, usually had a queue. The automated elevator fell into the 'ride at your own risk' category. An early rock group from London called The Teddy Boys entered the automated elevator one day with me and a tall man who had the stamp of transience about him. He pretended not to see The Teddy Boys who were less than conventional in appearance. But they were hugely good-natured and took my comment that the term Teddy Boy placed them rather far back in history without irritation, though they must have thought me pompous. With six of us in the small space the atmosphere was claustrophobic, but cheerful chatter alleviated this sensation until the elevator stopped abruptly between the seventh and eighth floors. The roof of the car hung just below the doors opening on to the eighth but our own door would not budge. Pushing the emergency button produced nothing. Shouting seemed not to be heard. Fifteen minutes passed and suddenly the tall man became hysterical. Hidden fear had surfaced, and he was desperate. The Teddy Boys tried to help, managing to force open the elevator door but there was nowhere the man could go without risking a fall down the shaft. This he seemed to be perfectly willing to countenance, seeing oblivion as a happy alternative to life temporarily suspended in the elevator, and he had to be restrained. Eventually we were freed, and from then on I waited for Purnell and his cynical smile. Better derision than claustrophobia. Purnell was at all times polite; but it was difficult not to sense his contempt. He sometimes overdid a servile manner which he must have learned at an early age was the best method of getting along in a white man's world. He was too old now to change.

In time, both elevators were automated which increased the general danger. Waits were longer because contrary to the theory that what goes up must come down, the elevators frequently resisted laws of gravity. Supposedly synchronized so that one would be up when the other was down, both elevators rose and fell together. Labouring under the exasperated thumping on buttons by impatient guests, they stubbornly stopped at every floor. For no apparent reason, they would go up when asked, even politely, to go down. When I recently returned to the Chelsea, I found the situation to be unchanged.

Tenants took their revenge. A sexual drawing, good enough for a rubbing, appeared on the brass trim of the left-hand elevator. It was removed to be replaced by graffiti less worthy of posterity: 'Toots and Apache'. This too was removed and a nostalgic 'Jean Cocteau' appeared. Also, 'Meanwhile . . .' No doubt the patient member of the staff who had been told to clean up the brass would have been Freddy. Freddy was a muscular Cuban with glasses. He worked mostly at night, prowling the floors, on the alert for fires, watching for danger, calling for lost cats, dragging out bodies, alerting the police – who arrived so often they were almost part of the tenancy.

When Stanley eventually moved me into Room 831, I began to make friends, friends who have stayed ever since. Little by little I began to understand the rare quality of the place where we could be ourselves without wariness or the sense of critical eyes. We could work and dream and even starve with the knowledge that we were not alone, or as far as it is possible not to be alone. A mutual and sometimes frenzied lack of inhibition prevailed, although for me this came later. At the start I was more circumspect as became a minor executive, a term that still sounds ridiculous. Stanley approved, however, and handed me the old-fashioned key to Room 831 (I still have it) with some ceremony. In subsequent years, I wondered if it was the MGM respectability that encouraged him where I was concerned, or the regular rent cheque. Both, probably. But when disaster struck and I joined the ranks of the impecunious, he still accepted me as a paid-up member of the Chelsea community.

My room was large with a double bed, a built-in closet, a desk too small to be of much use, armchairs, including the big original one in oak, and a dressing-table which, like the desk, belonged to the realm of cheap motel furniture. There was the 'Murphy' kitchen, a dining-room table and an ancient rug which I removed later to reveal beautiful floor boards. The bathroom – Thomas Wolfe's 'Throne Room' – was small, but it had a window. One could sit looking out at the Hudson, an inspiring and unusual view from a New York bathroom. There were the ubiquitous cockroaches too, but these did not put in an appearance until months later when my pedal-bin for garbage was accidentally left unemptied. The ensuing discovery of swarming, dark-brown, pulsating busybodies – I can never think of a cockroach with affection – drove me thenceforth to an almost neurotic cleanliness.

At my previous dwelling on York Avenue, there had been regular visits from an exterminator. He was a small man with a baseball cap and thick glasses which made him look like a housefly under a microscope. He went about his business without ceremony, flinging the occasional remark to me over his shoulder: 'Know what they're going to do? They're going to castrate all the male cockroaches.' This struck me as a worthwhile idea and I thought of it when invaded at the Chelsea. Here, though theoretically an exterminator was supposed to visit us regularly, as with so much about the Chelsea the visits remained theoretical unless Freddy or Jimmy the houseman felt inclined to make war.

The strangeness of my new home was mitigated largely by the staff, in particular the maid on my floor whose name was Irene. Like most of the staff, she was black and from the South, with a healthy cynicism, a regal bearing and huge kindness. She was also filled with curiosity about me, an American coming from England. I have a hunch that she regarded me as respectable because I had a job. Later, when I was jobless, her friendship proved to have depth. God knows what the maids said about us down in the bowels of their linen room, presided over then by a white housekeeper named Josie. Josie certainly showed no bigotry. If she had, it would have come to nothing, as sheer numbers would have defeated her. However, the staff, black and white, were unusually united. There were two reasons for this: low pay, and the unbelievable behaviour of the tenants, cause for gossip and mirth, enlivening a day that began in Harlem at five o'clock and ended in Manhattan at six in the evening with a long subway trip ahead.

Irene's part of the South was North Carolina. She often talked about her cooking and invited me to Sunday dinner at her home in Harlem. I could bring anyone I liked. I accepted for the future, not yet sure of my bearings, not yet having made intimate friends. Little by little they appeared, but it wasn't for several years that I managed my day out in Harlem.

The staff fleshed out and became familiar to me. I recognized that in their eyes we were mostly a kind of aberration of the genes, unless, of course, success touched us. They welcomed the casual way in which we lived, until it slopped over into the wild lack of concern in which rooms became almost uninhabitable, when the maids would squawk and clatter in the halls, conveying to one another their disapproval.

Integration, curiously, remained a problem in the Chelsea, although not always on the grounds of prejudice. It was a sense of old-fashioned, middle-class morality that prevailed, particularly among the women of

[28]

the staff. The frequent pimps were not discussed, at least not in our hearing. But Irene deeply disapproved of seeing any white girl with any black man. In reverse, there were occasional episodes in which whites mistook resident blacks for something they were not. I rode down in the elevator one day with a well-dressed matron, plainly someone passing through who no doubt had mistaken the Chelsea for something it was not. As we emerged in the lobby she called to a small black man standing nearby. He had an explosion of hair and colourful clothes. It was Jimi Hendrix.

Disregarding his appearance and lack of uniform – she seemed merely to have focused on the colour of his skin – she called, 'Boy, I need someone to bring down my bags!'

One of the world's greatest guitarists may have heard, but did not move. Intense embarrassment made nonsense of any explanation. I cannot remember what happened next; no doubt Percy or Purnell or Charles, all bona fide bellmen, appeared at just the right moment. The woman, watching television at some later date, might conceivably have recognized the small black musician smashing his guitar as the bellman who ignored her summons that day at the Chelsea. It seems doubtful.

It was sometimes said of Charles Beard, captain of the bellmen (though the haughty Purnell was senior in more subtle ways), that he was an Uncle Tom, that derogatory euphemism for blacks who ingratiate themselves with whites. Charles was in no way an Uncle Tom, although he sometimes went into a kind of soft-shoe shuffle routine with Purnell, a parody of Uncle Tom. Charles, in fact, was a man deeply concerned for the ill, the ageing and the lonely. His attitude was humanitarian in the Christian tradition. He often quoted from the Bible and had been a church warden.

The majority of the staff, like Irene, came from the South or the West Indies. Charles was a New Yorker, although his father, a longshore-man, did come from Virginia. When he was sixteen, Charles worked for a bakery for nine dollars a week plus tips. His mother had died, and there were eight sons and two daughters in the family. Before she died, Charles's mother taught her children to cook, sew, wash and iron, and Charles used his abilities when looking after some of his needy guests at the Chelsea. An all-round athlete as well as a boxer – featherweight at first, then welter-weight when he trained with Canada Lee – he moved briskly through all his tasks, looking after old ladies, feeding

[29]

pets temporarily deserted by their owners, trotting to hospital on errands for the ill or injured. Many guests had his home telephone number.

'You need me,' he said to me one day, genuinely distressed because I lived alone and was, he felt, in danger of falling ill and being unable to look after myself. He was right. It happened early one night. Ironically, Charles was not on duty. A sudden severe attack of hives paralyzed my lungs so that I was barely able to make it to the telephone to whisper 'doctor' before passing out. At the switchboard was Ruth Curley, slim and the colour of *café au lait*. She remembered that there did just happen to be a doctor in the house – though he was a surgeon and came reluctantly to my room along with a policeman. I was saved from imminent death by a large shot of adrenalin – so large that it produced a mild heart condition. This, though temporary, was none the less alarming, so I gave up smoking. Then, in the midst of my recovery, one of the new and very young bellmen stole my watch and the doctor, a Hungarian passing through New York, demanded his bill paid in full from the desk. Life, or trying to stay alive, did get complicated. The watch was quickly returned. As for me, more or less recovered after an ambulance trip to the Chelsea's home from home, St Vincent's Hospital, clad in nightgown and shapeless short coat provided by the hospital, I shuffled in large hospital slippers through the lobby at the Chelsea, praying that no one would be on hand to notice me getting out of the taxi and moving with all the care of a newborn being towards the elevators.

The lobby was empty and John Dorman, the night man, did not look up from his figuring. This did not mean to say he never looked up. On occasions, he had looked up and not liked what he saw. But there was a button under the desk conveniently connected with the police precinct.

The following morning, marvellously alive, I repaid the desk what it had given the doctor and walked into Stanley's office to explain, to apologize, to thank him – for the return of the watch – and, of course, to accept his commiseration on my unfortunate mishap.

He only looked at me from his youthful but weary chocolate-coloured Hungarian eyes and said: 'Why don't you get your jewellery insured?' He did not commiserate.

Jewellery! A thirty-dollar Timex which had been the gift of a friend freaked out on speed who had stolen it from a pawnbroker. On the way to work, adrenalin working, I mused about jewellery. Being presumed to possess it placed one in the category where reading the stockmarket reports or keeping a safe-deposit box are requisites of life. Ah, well. I wondered if Stanley knew how sweet his smile could be, and rather wished that he had smiled during our conversation. Jewellery and Hungarian smiles – it all belonged to the past when the trio played on the dais next to potted palms, and Lillian Russell was reflected in the plate-glass mirrors of the lobby. Looked at from another point of view, jewellery, even stolen Timex watches which are not insured, can make tiresome problems for the management. Charles Beard would have known this, without an explanation necessary. Which is one of the advantages of not being an artist.

Whatever the maids' considered, individual opinions may have been towards racism, they were collective in their discrimination against sexual injustice. A young black couple moved into a room on my floor, the eighth. The girl was pretty and flamboyant enough to bring a sniff or two from the more critical of the staff. The young man was excessively slim in very tight, high-waisted, bell-bottom trousers, gaudy, short sweaters and a many coloured velvet cap worn sideways on his hair which had been dyed red-gold. He had a fairish skin, and well-defined features. This couple fought, loudly and frequently. One would lock the other out, and vice versa. A day came when the noise augmented to the point that there were calls of complaint to the desk. The maids, however, had already taken a hand. Hanging at first to the banisters, tier on tier, or looking up from the stairwell below, they eventually converged on the angry twosome, adding their voices to the bedlam. They felt the girl was being bullied.

Epithets were exchanged, pointed and scatological. Then, abruptly, the whole thing died away. The management requested the pair to leave – but not before the maids had discovered the dyed-haired boy was in fact a girl.

Jesse tended the corridors. She was delicate and middle-aged, with an elegance that might well have fitted into the old Chelsea days with the mirrors and potted palms; or dancing in white gloves at the St Regis. But her face and bearing were very personal and belonged to whatever ambience welcomed her when the long day ended and, with her friends, green uniforms discarded and wigs stoutly in place, she set off for bus or subway.

At one time conversation in the corridors and in the elevators, which the maids often rode with the residents (the service elevator usually being out of order), was pithy and vibrant, whether it concerned sex, politics or the urgent business of survival. There was joy when the staff, maids, engineers and maintenance people alike, won their union-sponsored raise. A few were dismissed, this being the management's way of evening things up, and their regular rooms were no longer given service.

'Honey, you sure were looking down both barrels,' said one maid to another who had kept her job. Without practice or a quick ear, or a knowledge of what was in the wind, staff conversation could just as well be in code for the residents; unless, of course, certain of us were picked out for special attention, which is possibly why Irene extended her invitation to me. However, a lot of time passed before this happened; a lot of time, and a gradual build-up of trust and understanding.

Percy, who had taken my bags the first day, continued to utter malapropisms. He would never say no to a drink, which was rewarding because his sense of humour was diabolical. As he chatted away, he talked of feminine turts which it took me some time to translate as 'traits', and mentioned certain people as belonging to a certain 'categlory'. But he was wise and generous, and his love for his only son – an engineer in Colorado – encompassing and moving. His contempt for work amounted to a kind of *noblesse oblige* and eventually he was invited by Stanley to go on his way. I missed him, but knew he would probably be going out to Colorado to join his son.

A number of others came and went in his place. Gums, a chubby young West Indian, seemed bewildered and did not stay long; then another young man, who happened to be in the 'new' elevator when a cable snapped and he sank two floors at frightening speed. He never quite recovered from the shock, talked about it constantly and then left, presumably to talk about it elsewhere.

Down in the cellar, a huge and fascinating area filled with abandoned luggage, old furniture, trunks of letters and manuscripts – it was said – and a rat or two, there was a big, brightly lit and immaculate room where the hotel laundry was done in two enormous washing machines and a dryer. Audrey, the maid in charge, admitted that one of the washing machines, like the elevators, stopped working from time to time so the laundry had to be sent out. The walls of the room were white-washed and decorated only with two Breughel prints and a pornographic drawing of immense and enjoyable fornication.

[32]

This, said Doris, the other maid in the laundry, was the gift of a departed artist.

Just off the laundry was a small office where Josie the housekeeper presided. Small, attractive and white-haired, she was Irish and well able to dish out as much as she took, which was abundant. On affectionate terms with all the staff, who called her Jo, she knew where to look for someone missing, when to say 'no', when 'yes' and, at all times, when to stand up for her rights. Before one of Charles Beard's special friends, Miss Flynn, a legal secretary on the eighth floor, died in hospital, she would cook ham hocks and greens for all the Southern staff, being a Southerner herself. The bourbon would flow too, and it would become necessary for Josie to arrive and sort things out. Miss Flynn was large of girth, had false teeth and a warm heart. 'You'll see,' she told me after I lost my job. 'Things will get better. Ah know. Ah've been through it myself.'

When she was dying of diabetes, Charles visited Miss Flynn regularly and had to report sadly that she wanted him, against hospital regulations, to smuggle in extra food and a bottle of Jack Daniels. No doubt, save for the fact that he knew these would not help her condition, he would have obliged. 'She cheats a little,' he said with a smile of understanding.

The year after I arrived, Springer joined the staff as houseman. He was tall and grey-haired and proud of his work. He liked to finish things, objecting to pressure when the management sent him too quickly from one job to another. He, like Irene, was born and bred in North Carolina and, by his own word, closed his eyes to whatever he saw around him that was disconcerting. When I suggested to him that the Chelsea contained a portion of the world outside and therefore could not be judged in any other way, he nodded, all the time trying to scrape the black paint off a white bathroom sink.

'Yes, it's the people that makes the world,' he said. The oil paint was bothering him, and he only seemed to half-believe what he was saying. Probably an artist had put the paint there. A criterion is a sometime thing.

The engineers were overworked and often crabby. Besides Freddy, the night engineer, there was Jimmy, a youngish white man with a cheerful smile unless he felt put upon. There were two more Jimmies, both black; Rudy, a Filipino with glasses and a look of concern; and Prescott, whimsical and kind. All of these men seemed only too pleased to delegate authority, having other interests or preoccupations. Jimmy number two was very sexual, wore Bermuda shorts in summer, and loved women. He was not quite as sharp a dresser as Prescott, but he talked about sex at the drop of anyone's hat. It fascinated him, and on occasion he went beyond the limits of tact.

'You still like it, don't you?' he asked me persistently. 'I mean, you dig it, don't you? You got that feelin' . . .'

Jimmy number three was blue-black in complexion and carried about a sadness because of the recent death of his son. He played the horses with considerable success.

The front desk had a fairly rapid turnover. But the night man, John Dorman, seemed to be a fixture if only because one imagined it would take a derrick to move him. He had trained as an actor but was exceedingly big, a fact that made it difficult for him to get good parts. Before he came to work at the Chelsea, I had seen him in *Hogan's Goat* with Faye Dunaway at the American Place Theatre, and thought him talented. He himself did not like to be reminded of how excellent he was at his craft. 'It's the best-kept secret in New York,' he would say.

When I knew him first he was thirty-eight years old. Born in Boise, Idaho, he had fallen in love at an early age with Sally Rand, the fan dancer, and got his first newspaper job by discovering she was pregnant, apparently a scoop of importance on fan dancers' circuits. Several years elapsed, during which he played various roles in the Seattle Playhouse and was then taken on as a reporter for the *Pocatello* (Idaho) *Tribune*. He was Santa Claus at various times in various places, and then became a proof-reader but lost the job because he failed to see that 'six prancing horses' had emerged as 'six prancing whores'.

Despite the relative frequency of our visits from the precinct police, the front desk was not on the whole a dangerous place to be. The closest – in my time – that the Chelsea ever came to having a security guard was during the time of David in 1968. Black-haired, Jewish of feature, he was a young man who hung about the desk a great deal of the day or night. He had a slightly off-centre look, possibly the result of his calling and his oddly related passion for opera.

He said he was a locksmith and was given a small room in the cellar in which to fix the locks of guests who were ever prone either to break theirs or lose the keys. It can also be said that people other than guests broke down doors, possibly drugged on occasions, but also, one may be certain, offended somewhere within themselves that they were not the

ones to own the special key to open the special door. In fact hurt
feelings of all kinds were another reason for breaking down doors.
Gregory Corso, one of the last of the great Beat poets, rolled through
the hotel like a dark tumbleweed, managing to cadge a drink in passing
but announcing that 'just because you bought me a drink, Florence,
doesn't entitle you to talk to me'. So be it. Gregory: his moods
alternated between the demonic and the angelic. He could sit with a
lump of crystal in his hand and marvel at its perfection – or he could
exteriorize his feelings by kicking in a door. Another poet, Jerry
Benjamin, once invited me to his room to show me his poetry. I had not
been long back in my own room when he arrived in a temper that was
not only towering but atomic, kicked in the door and demanded his
poetry back, saying I had stolen it. In point of fact there was little to
steal, but their treatment of doors made one wonder about the
emotional climate of poets.

David therefore worked and watched. He appeared to be kind, once
driving me all the way to New Hampshire on my second visit to the
MacDowell Colony when I missed my bus. He was quiet, visited
people to listen to records sometimes, but mainly kept himself to
himself. Then one day, driving a new car – he always seemed to have a
different car – he disappeared. Police were called and broke into his
room. They found a fairly substantial arsenal of all kinds of weapons
and ammunition as well as stolen items such as radios, toasters,
tape-recorders, for which he had allegedly been 'hunting'. The largest
haul, of $50,000 worth of jewellery belonging to an affluent transient
(that is, not a long-term resident), was not there. Neither David nor the
jewellery were ever seen again, at least within Chelsea walls.

The switchboard operators had one of the most arduous jobs in the
house. Indeed, some found their health breaking down under the
manic, winking lights, the octopus cords, and the irate demands of
residents unaware of the difficulty of handling dozens of incoming and
outgoing calls on a single switchboard. Today all that is modernized, to
a point, yet it seems possible that even a computer might collapse at
the Chelsea. The human factor is ever present.

Back then there were moments of violence when callers, tried
beyond patience, came downstairs to attack verbally the operator who
appeared to be responsible. On one such occasion a white girl, having
failed to receive a message concerning a vitally important business
appointment, screamed abuse over the desk and was slashed across her

face with a Coke bottle by the statuesque black operator who was not one of our regulars.

Verbal assaults which were racist in tone, even if founded on extreme exasperation due to carelessness, obviously ran the risk of being returned with physical retaliation. Mostly, however, it was impotent fury, expressed in different ways from one resident to another, which reigned when the switchboard was busy or the lone operator had to go to the bathroom, leaving the lights to flash and the board to buzz to no avail.

A typical case was as follows, overheard during my later days at the Chelsea when I had learned patience in these matters. Lines were perpetually being crossed.

A male voice, slightly accented by middle-Europe: 'May I have long distance please, operator?'

A second male voice, young and American: 'I'm not the operator.'

Spoken together, in ominous duet, 'Hello, hello, operator.'

'Please get off my line!' This from the man with the accent.

The American's tone was building to outrage. 'Sorry, snot-nose.' His sarcasm sounded merely childish.

Again the 'Hellos' in unison, followed by a brief, breathing silence. The European tried again. 'Please may I be connected with long distance?'

A triumphant laugh from the American. 'Long distance isn't working for you.'

Both men still seemed under the impression that there really was an operator, which there was not.

'Get off!'

'No, you get off!' The American was reaching hysteria. 'Faggot! Creep! Son-of-a-bitch!'

Down below more lights must have flashed as the breathing silence was invaded again, this time by feminine voices. The first was French, sweet, polite, firm.

''allo, 'allo, zis iz zee operateur?'

'No,' said a young American girl's voice. 'I'm looking for her too.'

Laughter. The girls began chatting but were stopped short when the American man said, 'Hello, what I'm looking for is a *ménage à trois*.'

This brought further silence until a fifth, feminine and angry voice crashed through a burgeoning flirtation.

'For God's sake why don't you wear a dress instead of pants!'

For whom the remark was intended is anybody's guess. But it contained such scorn, such frustration, that I was embarrassed and hung up quietly, knowing from long experience that there was no point in attempting to put a call through the switchboard for some time.

Whenever this happened, Stanley Bard was besieged with complaints, even from his employees. But they were all lost in the wind of Stanley's passing as he hurried away on other sudden business. Until the switchboard was mended, the Chelsea would be cut off from the world.

Queen of the switchboard operators, though extremely modest, was Josephine Brickman, a handsome woman with beautiful thick white hair and a liking for brightly coloured dresses. Nothing disturbed her or her sense of humour. She was efficient, having been a telephone operator with the Wacs during World War Two. She had been shipped to England and, through a mix-up in orders, found herself at a British base where she was the only woman among thousands of GIs and Air Force pilots. A cheer went up when she stepped out of the car. She spent the night in the officers' quarters, chastely, and was driven to her proper assignment in the back of an officer's car. She loved to tell this story. We enjoyed listening to it, imagining 'The White Cliffs of Dover', Vera Lynn, Glenn Miller and GI brides. Being the right age for it all, I remembered better than most.

As a civilian operator Josephine could run to ground any resident who was in or within reach of the hotel simply through the method of intelligent deduction. She was her own private detective agency. She was also well aware of union rules, and objected rightly if an amateur took over when she was absent. A cord twisted out of place, a metal cap loosened, affected her much as the mindless writing of someone on the inside cover of a signed first edition. The switchboard was her tenure where expertise and training were in constant evidence, apart, of course, from the moments of the frequent mechanical breakdowns. 'Thank God! Josephine's back!' was the cry after one of her infrequent vacations.

Other operators were adequate enough but made mistakes, like being absent at crucial moments such as the time of a holdup, something that happened perhaps twice a year. All the desk clerks and switchboard operators were subject to crime wandering in off the streets and, despite the police button under the desk, there were

[37]

hair-raising moments when it was out of order. A knife flashed, the till was emptied, the staff stayed rigid with fear.

In the winters the radiators clanked and murmured like the radiators in all old buildings, but they kept the warmth and a nostalgia that is peculiarly American. Air-conditioners were not supplied and the hot New York summer nights offered little possibility of sleep. Yet I managed without air-conditioning for three years, until I received a unit as a Christmas present. It sat there on my floor − on Thomas Wolfe's floor − looking alien. I wondered what to do. Installing private air-conditioners was non-union work and that made a problem. Help was at hand.

Chris Moyes, a young Englishman who came in off my fire-escape one day wearing one earring, and who remained a close friend, offered to do it. Chris was ingenious. When he worked and was not being a gypsy, he had a job as messenger for the British Consulate and had recently begun drawing Modigliani-like heads in ink on the mail bags containing classified information. Summoned to head office, he felt his time had come, but did not care, having decided anyway to go to New Mexico. To his astonishment, his boss congratulated him, said there had been messages of admiration from all points, but added that Chris really should start using paint as it would be more effective.

Soon after this, Chris got a job with Cristo − the artist who wraps landscapes − and who also lived on and off at the hotel. Chris arrived at the Chelsea ahead of his employer to supervise and care for the vast quantities of material used in Cristo's work.

He felt he might need help with the air-conditioner and I agreed, having visions of it crashing to the synagogue roof below my window. Next door, a new guest had recently arrived, a spare, black-haired young man always dressed in dark trousers and white shirt. He once told me he would like to call. Chris and I enlisted his help. The air-conditioner thus brought Bertolt Brecht's son Stefan into my life. Stefan is still at the Chelsea, living now in room 1010, where Edgar Lee Masters used to stay.

The advent of new technology, including, besides police buttons, air-conditioners, stereos and coloured TV sets, put a heavy load on the rest of the antiquated electrical system of the hotel. However, by Stanley Bard's calculations, thrift was to be valued above securing the world against possible dangers, or at least an effort has to be made to combine the two, even if it might mean one would cancel out the other.

[38]

For example, on the fifth floor there was a fuse box at floor level that was given to overheating during the warm days of summer. To prevent, or at least to alleviate, this condition, an ancient black fan, groaning and rattling, played cool air on the fuses. The box was situated behind an old church pew that came from God knows, if He knew, where. On this pew residents sat exhaustedly while awaiting recalcitrant elevators. The pew had been pulled away from the wall and the fan chained to a water pipe in the manner that motorcycles are chained and padlocked by their owners to fire hydrants or railings. There was no doubt that one day some unconcerned resident, finding his room too warm, would try to steal the fan. If he pulled the waterpipe too hard, there would be a flood, which meant the fire department and short circuits. Such an accident was not only possible but probable, given this Rube Goldberg/Heath Robinson invention. But the arrangement itself was somehow very Chelsean. Furthermore, considering the initial solidity of the hotel's structure, it would have been of enormous expense and difficulty to rewire the building.

Wherever possible, the Chelsea moved with the times. That it also declined with the times was of no real importance if one loved the place, as we did.

'It is home,' said Marguerite Gibbons, painter and ballerina who had lived in a penthouse apartment for thirteen years. And Charles James, one of the world's great and unjustifiably forgotten couturiers, asked if he was glad he moved into the Chelsea in 1965 said, 'Good God, yes; where else could I live and dress as I want?'

[39]

THREE

EL QUIJOTE

IN my room I had an oven which was adequate, but I did little cooking until MGM and I parted company. This would not be until 1970. Meanwhile there was money to spend on meals, and many of these I took, when less affluent after paying Stanley my monthly $200, at the corner Horn and Hardart chain cafeteria.

Horn and Hardart, scarcely above the greasy-spoon type of restaurant, self-service and packed with tables, was yet regarded by most Chelseaites as the Café Dome, the Coupole, the Closerie des Lilas of Twenty-Third Street. Many decisions were made over the dreary tables and cups of cooling coffee that, poured from dripping, rococo taps that never stopped running until the cup overflowed, left a pool of liquid to be sopped up by paper napkins. Yet here, amid the lonely old men; the lonely young men from the McBurney YMCA across the street from the Chelsea; amid the ageing trollops with their shopping bags of nameless contents; the odd businessmen in a hurry and on a pinched expense account; here some of the distinguished artists of the world plotted and inspired one another.

'Aaron Copland, Marc Blitzstein and I drew up the plans for a co-operative music press open to all composers whose music we should find acceptable,' wrote Virgil Thomson in his autobiography. The meeting, he wrote, took place 'in an Automat near my hotel'.

Horn and Hardart was one of William Burroughs's pet working spots, and film-makers, writers, musicians, have all carried their trays to the cash register usually presided over by a large, shapeless girl with ferret eyes, certainly the equivalent of those black-draped, corseted women who still preside, but more rarely now, over the *caisses* in the cafés of Saint-Germain-des-Pres.

The food was decidedly less than superlative, but it nourished. My great friend Charles James always dined at Horn and Hardart when out of funds, which was mostly. One night he arrived to discover that the last piece of steak had been taken by a policeman who was in line ahead of him. Charles was outraged. 'But I always dine here,' he said in his elegant way. At that moment, Horn and Hardart could well have been the Tour d'Argent or Prunier, but there was no *maitre d'* and Charles went without his steak that night.

After Off-Track Betting opened one of its offices near the Chelsea, those who followed the races met for breakfast with other racing fans in a kind of undeclared club at tables set close together in Horn and Hardart. They discussed the chances in the day's races; talked of past wins; mourned losses; studied forms.

The charm of the old Automat days, when one could put coins (originally a nickle) in a slot and watch with childish pleasure as a small door opened allowing access to sandwiches, wedges of pie, or whatever one desired, is gone. Now, although attempts to improve the place have been made from time to time, it is purely cafeteria style. The process of improvement began perhaps inauspiciously with an advertising campaign, 'Our Spinach Is Good For Your Tired Feet', evoking lurid images of treading in green slime rather than, one supposes, a comfortable chair where one could rest one's feet while at the same time eating spinach. There was also the somewhat sibylline utterance: 'The First Woman Who Comes in Wearing Purple Shoes Gets a Free Slice of Blueberry Pie'. These advertisements then dwindled and radical re-decoration took their place. Half-timbering appeared; boxes of artificial flowers bloomed in leaded windows. The quality of the food, however, remained unchanged. Later, further transformations took place. The Automat became a disco on Saturday nights, being solely for blacks who arrived from uptown by bus. The curtains were drawn across the windows, but the music with its inviting beat jumped out into the street causing query and some chagrin as to why a 'blacks only' spot had come into being on Twenty-Third Street, which is as about as integrated as any thoroughfare in Manhattan.

Around the corner from Horn and Hardart, on Seventh Avenue, was the Angry Squire, owned by a former ship's steward, Frank Godin, from Liverpool. Frank was very English and very knowing. Red-haired, with a thick scouse accent, he was an ambitious proprietor, trying all kinds of innovations, which ranged from jazz piano to 'navel' contests involving young women who paraded with bared midriffs. Aware of the importance of feminine pulchritude, Frank also understood the need for men, British and American, to stand in groups, get drunk, talk sport and then, gradually, or immediately, sex. He set a good table, all British-type food down to his shepherd's pie. Chelsea residents frequented the Angry Squire despite its one glaring draw-back, that Frank was unwilling to cash cheques. Yet he had moments of generosity and once broke open a bottle of champagne on my birth-day.

Other dining places in the immediate area were the Sancho Panza, which old-timers still called the Anchor Inn, and the Blarney Stone, again usually referred to by its original name of the Oasis. The Blarney Stone was of course Irish and the drinks were cheaper than in other bars in the neighbourhood. Food was abundant and cheap: Hungarian goulash, cabbage, huge helpings of pastrami, steak sandwiches, and so on. A lot of Chelsea people ate their main meal of the day there. For me it was a place of guaranteed instant heartburn. But I was there, with a friend, a Belgian painter, the night they made the first moon-landing. The television set, usually given over to baseball or football or soap opera, was tuned in, and offered abominable reception. No one cared. The breathless moment when the first man would set foot on the moon approached. There was absolute silence. But only for a moment. At the far end of the bar, near the door, three old men completely indifferent to what was happening squabbled among themselves in loud voices as to which owed another fifty cents. Strangely, no one shushed them. But then, what use to them would a moon-landing be? Whereas fifty cents could go far towards a bottle of Ripple, the gut-destroying wine they drank. The curious aspect of the case was that they must have been feeling affluent to have been drinking at the Blarney Stone. Possibly the answer lay in that they had come in originally to watch the moon-landing; then, with alcohol awash in their brain-cells, forgotten all about it.

The Blarney Stone was very much more of a neighbourhood bar than the others we attended. Opening at eight in the morning, it was a fine spot for the first drink of the day. At that time of day, the drinkers seemed to dislike company. I would see hung-over friends pretending not to notice one another as they left the hotel, setting off determinedly in opposite directions. The Sancho Panza was very Spanish and specialized in sea-food, with live lobsters clicking about in a tank in the window. The manager was a stocky, good-looking young Spaniard with graceful manners. His barmaid looked like an excep-tionally beautiful American Indian with a trace of Chinese. Yet she too was Spanish. The clientele was mainly Spanish and physically on the small side. They came in male batches to sit in a row at the short bar, reminding one of the Paddy Chayevsky film where the young men keep asking one another: 'Whaddayou gonna do?' 'I don't know. Whaddayou gonna do?'

At the Sancho Panza the action started late, and usually involved dancing to a flamenco guitar. The small bar was pleasantly dim, but the brightly-lit dining room offered no place to hide, if one was so inclined. This was unlike the Angry Squire, which was candlelit at the back tables and so dark, in fact, that the food was not always wholly discernible. That called for trust. But the dark was excellent for the ageing and the lovers.

Across Twenty-Third Street from the Chelsea was Pippins where girls in leotards served squalid tables. Pippins was popular late at night and people gathered to drink coffee, talk and watch the girls.

Also open late at night was George's Delicatessen, a small building that was almost a part of the Chelsea walls. George, a Greek, made good sandwiches and his manner while cutting roast beef or smearing mustard on a ham roll suggested a tough British sergeant. 'Hup, hup, hurry it up now!' he would shout. He was in his way indispensable for late eaters.

Cavanaugh's, just down the street from the Chelsea, had once been one of the more elegant restaurants in New York. It still served certain superlative dishes and the waiters, all elderly, would put a bottle of Scotch on the table from which the diner could help himself. But Cavanaugh's was for special occasions: the sale of a book or painting, entertaining visiting notables, celebrating a birthday if a birthday cheque was also in evidence.

For nearly everyone, however, it was the Spanish restaurant next door which had taken over one of the Chelsea's original dining rooms, El Quijote, which was the main gathering place. Even for the penniless: one could almost always scrounge a drink, or a small dish of black beans.

The restaurant was − and is − reached by a hall running from the area by the front desk of the hotel. A glass door is kept locked except at opening time, around noon − for lunches − and in the late afternoon. The locking-up was arbitrary in my time. If there had been a fracas the night before, if the waiters and Manolo the manager were tired, cynical, fed-up, the door was locked. This did not worry most of us. We used the door leading to the street. Long afternoons were spent over a beer or a sangria. Manolo and his staff were forbearing. Some of my most peaceful times were spent in El Quijote, usually alone if it was afternoon, sitting at the bar on a red leatherette-upholstered stool, listening to Frank Sinatra singing 'Strangers in the Night' or, if the music was silent, to the gentle splashing of water behind the bar — water in which the glasses were rinsed but which sounded like mountain brooks.

There were three owners of El Quijote in my day: José (Felix) Rodriguez, Gilbert Otero and Manuel Maino, or Manolo. All three came from Galicia in north-west Spain, though each had lived many years in New York and they had owned the restaurant for over twenty years. The kitchens where José, tall and gently handsome, presided were the original Chelsea kitchens with minor changes. But he and his partners had found it all too expensive to re-open all the dining rooms where the gentry of the Gay 'Nineties had dined, save for the one mentioned before, where there were birthday parties, political meetings, weddings, almost all Spanish affairs.

Manolo ran the bar with Pepe, a Cuban fisherman's son, as his assistant. Pepe was either merry to the point of detonation or wholly irresponsible, acting as though he could not give a Cuban damn for anyone. But his sense of fun was always uppermost and, although pragmatic, he was well known for suddenly filling up one's glass for free just because he felt like it. The position of bartender was interchangeable with two or three of the waiters and young Gilbert, Gilbert Otero's son who had been learning the business ever since he was discharged from the Marines. But this interchange only occurred when both Pepe and Manolo were away. Best of the substitutes was Arturo, a wise, twinkling man from Peru. Running him second were Juan, a very dark and heavily good-looking Argentinian, and Carols, a Cuban like Pepe who, after he grew a white moustache, resembled a Spanish don. Last came another Manuel, a genuine Spanish Gypsy and highly temperamental.

Gilbert the elder, always *soigné* and elegant in tailored suits, greeted diners and conducted them to their tables. He had eyes like glistening chestnuts and a certain *savoir-faire* which he did not always exert when the diners were from the Chelsea and on the level of a cup of *caldo gallego*, or a hamburger, Spanish style. Yet he did lend money in times of stress and was generally a most considerate man.

Spaniards, or those who were well-heeled, lunched or dined in a long, leisurely fashion. But a Chelseaite was more often than not in a state of penury and it might have been sheer defiance that sent him into El Quijote instead of the pizza joint or the delicatessen where he belonged. Gilbert, eyes busy, had come to know over the years all the Chelsea regulars. The successful, or those who had just received their welfare or unemployment cheques, arrived with self-confidence to receive the correct attention of a well-trained restauranteur. Others, aware there would be no ceremony for them, usually seated them-selves, thankfully, in a corner where they were often forgotten.

But it is only fair to say that discrimination was not especially financial. Manolo was capable of patience and generosity and, like Gilbert, lent money and allowed tabs to mount up. Neglect was less discriminatory than the result of waiters going into a trance, immobi-lized by some strange short-circuit in time. They dreamed and were still. Service, if there was any to start with, ceased. No silver was brought, no tablecloth, no napkins, no water, no menu. But this immobility applied to all comers, not just to those of the Chelsea; to the well-dressed as to the sloppy. It must have something to do with the changes in the moon, or an enormous boredom; or a mysterious Spanish introspection, Spanish indigestion, Spanish *mañana*. The trance could generally only be ruptured by Manolo or big Garcia snapping tableclothes into place as though wielding bullfighters' capes. Movement began; water was poured; and food began to arrive from the kitchen. Occasionally the hiatus was sparked off by baseball, which was preferred even to Spanish music from the juke box. All − Galicians, South Americans, Puerto Ricans, Cubans − shared a respect for baseball. When Joe di Maggio wandered through the bar he was mobbed. And everyone was thankful that Arthur Miller, dining there as he often did, had just left.

Pepe even kept a baseball bat under the counter, used as a threat for unruly customers, but flourished with a smile. In any case, it was big Gilbert who handled the difficult drinkers, frog-marching them to the door in his beautiful suit, elaborate tie and shirt and white shoes. White shoes seemed to be peculiarly Spanish. Pepe, when off-duty, wore them, as did Juan, and Bobby Capo, a handsome Puerto Rican singer who frequented the bar.

Bobby was an El Quijote regular and hugely respected. His amiably corrupt good looks were frequently lit up by a warm smile and he was usually accompanied by one nubile girl or another whose hair flowed in a black river almost to her coccyx. When the girls were present,

[45]

there was much staring and muffled comment from the waiters. The female was important, but in her rightful place, in the home and as a pleasant adjunct to male superiority. Most Spaniards, whether true-blue from Spain, or Spanish descendants from other countries, had to be given the unhappy label of male chauvinism.

The Chelsea had inevitably rubbed off on El Quijote. The waiters and management had, at last, over the years come to accept the fact that a woman alone did not necessarily come to pick up a man. Nor was she a prostitute. She was merely a woman, they were forced to admit, who was lonely and wanted a drink and some conversation. Yet, at the same time, El Quijote had never fully accepted the Chelsea residents in their alternate deliberate shabbiness, or dangling cut-out *outré* hippie garments. The staff could not be persuaded into accept-ance, nor could they be bludgeoned, even by Andy Warhol and his Chelsea Girls when they were dining regularly at El Quijote. When Janis Joplin, with her ostrich plumes, beads and ribbons, held big dinner parties, the waiters watched with stunned expressions. They valiantly served food at a long table with Allen Ginsberg in his prayer shawl at one end and Leonard Cohen in his element – usually with two or more teenaged maidens – at the other, both shouting of the profits they had made on their poetry. In between sat Harry Smith, the underground film-maker, like a hunched George Washington, his thick grey hair tied with a black ribbon; Mary Beach (who was related to Sylvia Beach, confidante to Paris's 'Lost Generation' and publisher of James Joyce); and somewhere along the table I held my place and watched in fascination. All of us were able to understand the vibrancy of the talk and the calculated vulgarity, but it is highly doubtful if the waiters could. They continued to serve food with an air of bemusement, excellent *paella Quijote*, seldom seafood *al Jerez*, because it was expensive, frequently *picadillo à la Creole*, a comforting mixture of ground meat, peppers, rice and black beans, sangria and wine. Gert Schiff, art historian, and one of the few Chelsea residents given to suits and homburg hats, was there eating a splendid thick soup, *gazpacho Andaluz*. William Burroughs sipped wine, at the same table, solemn as an undertaker, and watchful.

Whatever their opinions, the staff and management of El Quijote were always fascinated by what happened in the Chelsea. And there had been considerable fraternization that passed well beyond the admiring pinch, the puckered lips of a silent kiss or a furtive caress.

There was at least one small, very beautiful child trotting down the marble halls of the Chelsea whose father was a waiter, proud of his calling, his race and his paternity.

For me El Quijote was always a good place in which to think. When I was no longer employed by MGM, when I had time to spare, it was another kind of refuge. There was quiet after the lunchtime crowd had gone. The sound of water ran beneath the bar counter, but otherwise the early afternoons were silent. There may have been one or two other regulars, like Henry Gould, a former World War Two pilot, slim and even-featured. Henry was quiet unless drunk, but usually managed to contain his drinking. He, like one or two others in the afternoon hours, sat with his own thoughts. A late luncher, possibly discussing a film project with a companion, would order capuccino, and a sulky waiter, noting it was within a few minutes of two when all lunch service stopped, would start making it. The machine, picking up his thought wave, would break down. Milk would shoot in all directions, and the client would settle for American coffee. The luncheon would end and the silence, water-filled, descend. I would sit looking up, as I had looked for eight years, at the woodcarvings of Don Quijote and Sancho Panza; of deer and wine bottles; cardboard figures tilting at windmills; huge cut-outs manufactured by young Gilbert, and containing a charm of their own; a silver cup, said to have been donated to Manolo for his ability to make love; the beaked wine bottles for real drinkers known as *pour – ons*; photographs of parties; the heavy red curtains; the beloved television set. The wallpaper was faded red, with a pattern of Don Quijote and his faithful Sancho repeated over and over.

I remember one evening when the painter John Hultberg, deep in his cups, decided to take offence, or at least to offer an indignant Manolo some of the resentment he felt, at a decor so insistently Spanish. John ripped off a piece of the – to him – offending wallpaper, shouting that Manolo would not know what a real artist was. To which Manolo replied, with a patience veiling anger, that a bartender must show his clients that he knew Goya and Velasquez.

'I'd believe you if you told me their first names,' said John.

Then the argument petered out. Hultberg was close to his lying-down period of the evening and Manolo knew it. It was more difficult for him to accept criticism from the painter Julio de Diego, a fellow Spaniard who found Manolo's decor in outrageous bad taste and declared it utterly bogus. Julio, who had once been married to Gypsy

[47]

Rose Lee, the famous striptease artist, was one of those who left the Chelsea and moved to Woodstock. We were great friends and from time to time he returned, drinking in El Quijote at these times, though I think Manolo never really forgave him.

As time moved towards the cocktail hour, other human oddments would pass through, like Zoa, a young man of indeterminate calling, his hair in wild snarls and his garments giving him the appearance of a Vietnam veteran. If no one he needed was in the bar, he moved on. More Spaniards would arrive. Pepe would drift in. The evening was about to start. Talk proliferated, all in Spanish but with sentences inevitably ending in an emphatic American 'Right!'

If the evening promised to be a full one, there were 'reserved' signs placed on various tables, and couples began to arrive. They all looked overfed. The women wore bright pant suits in summer and winter. Almost invariably their hair had been 'done'. There was much handshaking, much laughter. Chelsea people, coming in to seek each other, retreated.

We tended to stay away, too, on those occasions when the atmosphere at El Quijote seemed to crystallize into a purely Spanish one, such as Sundays when it was 'family' night and small children, all rather beautiful, ran about the restaurant. For one thing, the roast beef, a speciality of the Sunday meal together with champagne cocktails, was in short supply and kept for the occasional diner or for those whose bills had been paid regularly. 'Roderick got roast beef,' someone would say bitterly, wondering why Roderick deserved it.

Spanish Sundays were, in the vernacular of the day, 'heavy'. The juke box played 'Happy Birthday', the more obvious Spanish tunes, Frank Sinatra inevitably singing the ubiquitous 'Strangers in the Night', the attractive 'Girl From Ipanema' or 'Man of La Mancha'.

On some evenings a great intermingling occurred. Not on the more expected occasions like Christmas or New Year, when paper hats, horns and streamers were brought into play. No, these heterogeneous times happened by chance, and they were joyful. Spaniards knew how to enjoy themselves. There was kissing and goodwill and a random sexuality. Drinks were suddenly on the house. Bookkeeping went to hell.

There was a 'Spaniards for Nixon' night at the time of his last election. I waited doggedly throughout to see what would happen, having just voted the Democratic ticket. A card table was set up

[48]

outside the spare dining room with its dark red, gold-looped curtains. Girls with low-cut dresses and straw boaters sat handing out leaflets. There were small American flags everywhere. The waiters ran about, busy, busy, busy. There was a great confraternity of waistcoats among them, a substitute for the conventional waiter's jacket. That night they appeared to be more elaborate than ever. Brocaded, with satin backs, they were indeed beauteous. Big Gilbert was the only one who never wore a waistcoat.

Nothing happened at the Nixon night. He won.

,Summers were quiet times, for the most part, though on extremely hot nights the clients arrived in great numbers, with people three deep in the cool bar. Quiet times were best. Over the years, the regulars came and went. Some disappeared for months, to reappear abruptly. Manolo had worked for years on the boats of the United Fruit Company and had a special affection for seamen, who turned up from time to time. But where could one place Ernie, a 'super' or janitor, from a building across the street?

It was difficult to guess his age – about forty, perhaps. In his green work clothes and brown shoes, he could come into El Quijote and settle down for another beer, obviously having called in at a number of other bars en route. One day he saw me taking notes, as ever.

'Scratching away, always scratching,' he said nastily.

Manolo, hovering, said with a touch of warning, 'Ernie . . .'

Ernie subsided, but a moment later he was expressing his disgust for Spaniards who had lived most of their lives in the United States but still felt they must express themselves in Spanish.

Ernie was European with a trace of accent – German Jewish, I decided. Manolo told me he thought Ernie's family had died in a concentration camp, but because Ernie, unless drunk, was reticent, one could only guess the details. Then, one night when he was very drunk, he told me how he had tried to write. He looked at me with wavering dark eyes and said, 'Oh, Florence, you should have been born in a box car.'

There was some Fascism hovering in the air of the bar, but with that remark the SS walked in. Not long after this, Ernie was ejected for making a scene. I told Manolo of his remark and Manolo went very quiet because he understood and because he could be compassionate.

Two or three times a month a trio of Spanish students entered the bar and, dressed in classical Spanish style with capes and ribbons, sang and played tepidly on mandolin, accordion and nothing else. Once upon a time they were very good, but over the years their appearance seemed to become an increasingly commercial venture. Originally there was a dais holding a grand piano, but in my years this was never used save by drunken customers. There was, however, a series of guitar players, one of whom dared play 'Los Cuatros Generales' on request (mine). Then these too vanished, together with the dais. A Greek sold flowers to the diners, orchids for show-offs, large single roses for the amorous or intoxicated. He was a man of heart. I rode a bus with him one evening coming away from a horrible scene in Times Square where a man had fallen in front of a train. The flower seller must have noticed my expression because, without speaking, he handed me a rose.

From time to time, like a reminder of human frailty, a deaf mute appeared, distributing cards which read: 'Pardon me, I am a deaf mute.' I was never quite certain what he expected us to do. I'm certain we pardoned him; he seemed quite cheerful.

Manolo, father of eight with one child adopted, had every right to leave his paternal feelings at home when he came to El Quijote. The Chelsea 'family' was not always endearing. They sat for hours over a Coca-Cola, or fell about drunkenly. They threw wine in one another's faces on occasions, or tumbled from their stools into another world.

Incidents of this nature, wine-throwing and the behaviour of junkies and ordinary residents alike, did not endear the Chelsea to the El Quijote. At the same time there were other regulars from the hotel who mixed well enough with the outsiders. Scratch a businessman and you find a Sunday painter.

FOUR

THE SIXTIES – MUSIC AND HAPPENINGS

COMPOSERS at the Chelsea seem to have been in short supply through the years. Virgil Thomson was and is the king of them. However, another composer, of a different type but of equal importance in his own way, lived above Virgil in a penthouse apartment on the tenth floor. This was George Kleinsinger whose lovely musical *Shinbone Alley*, with Eartha Kitt as Mehitabel, might not have rated internationally as high as Virgil's *Four Saints in Three Acts*, but whose popularity was extensive. George was altogether an adorable man: eccentric, charming, always in love and devoted to women and animals.

His penthouse studio swarmed with free-flying birds, flashing blue and scarlet as they flew or hopped from perch to perch. Romantics loved them. The more pragmatic dodged the 'liquid siftings' – as T.S. Eliot put it – of mynah bird, toucanette, thrush, strange little jungle birds and parrot. But everyone felt the enchantment of the man.

George's Chinese nightingale was drab in comparison with the more exotic birds until it opened its beak to emit a cascade of pearl and crystal notes. With only one small representative of the species, George could not suggest T.S. Eliot's Sweeney Among the Nightingales, qualifying better for J. Alfred Prufrock in that he was old enough to 'keep my trousers rolled'. In all the years I knew him, his youthful spirit prevailed and he was always ready to 'eat a peach'. Unlike Prufrock, however, George knew that the mermaids, the kind with legs, would never fail to sing to him. If it had been possible he would have undoubtedly kept one in his biggest fish tank.

At one memorable time, George kept a huge toucan with a rainbow-coloured beak. It occupied its own private cage as befitted a bird of dignity. Whenever George had a musical evening, which was often, the toucan would watch with one eye while a piano quartet rendered Beethoven, then begin at a carefully selected moment to

[51]

clack its beak like a metronome, keeping ruthlessly to its own rhythm and causing the musicians to stumble and lose their way.

This animal participation was not restricted to the toucan only. George owned two monkeys which were sometimes affected by the music to the point of hysteria, making flying leaps from the backs of chairs to people's shoulders. It is unnerving to find oneself sharing a gin and tonic with a spider monkey, obviously bent on quelling its excitation by becoming thoroughly intoxicated.

In his youth, George had had other ambitions than that of being a composer. He had first decided to become a dentist, but after he was well into his studies, his teacher, J. Robert Schumacher, one of the faculty at Northwestern University Dental School, persuaded George to return to his earliest passion. In 1973, after watching a television programme in which George was featured, Dr Schumacher, now living in Alabama, wrote to say how happy he was to have discouraged George in his choice of a professional career in dentistry. The letter was also in answer to George's 'Thank you', written twenty-four years later.

'Since reading that letter,' wrote the dentist, 'I have seen your name on many TV programs and I have been very proud that I played a small role in these successes.'

By then, George had many successes to his credit. Besides the well-known *Tubby the Tuba*, a symphony narrated for children − Danny Kaye's being the most popular version, and played all over the world − there were many excellent compositions including a cello concerto, the stirring 'Sabre Dance' and many more. George was always in demand for TV commercials, most of them better than average, but one of his most interesting moments on television involved a short piece of music incorporated in a documentary on Leonardo da Vinci. It was Gert Schiff, an art historian who had lived at the Chelsea for years − a Swiss-German by birth − who discovered the music in a drawing by da Vinci. George, using a mirror to decipher the notes, which had been drawn backward, played it on his piano, wrote down the piece and presented the score to CBS.

When I first met George he was on the verge of a second marriage, to the dismay of his mermaids. The wife he chose, or who chose him, was named Kate and she stalked the halls prettily with a pewter goblet of gin in one hand. Sadly, George's marriage to Kate did not last long. When the end was in sight, Kate razed George's studio to the floor, hacking at the grand piano, tearing up papers, smashing the little

[52]

waterfall George kept for its sweet melody. A no-man's land after this attack, the room presented much of interest to the underground film-maker Harry Smith, whose abiding fascination for garbage heaps, cluttered shop windows and demolition sites, and other natural domiciles of detritus has resulted in an ongoing documentary, possibly even now not finished. Carefully and methodically he photographed the wreckage of George's room and it is probably now part of his long, painstakingly edited film.

But George recovered, replacing what had been destroyed with new furniture and new pets like the spider monkeys. When these proved too destructive George gave them away. He also removed his snakes, including the python which, brought from its cage to be shown off, liked to wrap itself around waists and shoulders like a cold rubbery arm. The boa constrictor's ingurgitation of its regular diet of live white mice was a sight for sadists.

Snakes, monkeys and a large colourful parrot disposed of, the big toucan sadly dying of old age, there remained, apart from many exotic fish, George's beloved long-necked Amazon turtle, swimming like an underwater ballet unto itself as the music played. The iguanas also stayed the course, though smaller lizards died of unknown causes.

The once teeming animal population was further reduced as George's interests turned more to plants and trees for his pleasure. In the corner by the waterfall a very tall tree managed to stay alive, although his sightless white catfish perished when something went amiss with the mechanism of the water-flow and George did not notice. A coot which he had rescued one cold winter night when it landed on his skylight, and which had escaped inspection from two stern officials of the ASPCA by being hidden in a friend's room, throttled itself in a wire milk-crate. The nightingale sang itself to death, and the rarest of his collection, a kind of turtle called a matamata that resembled some prehistoric rock, also gave up the ghost. After his death, Madeleine — a favoured mermaid — bought George another, not an easy task since matamatas are in short supply. But after a search one was found at a shop unfortunately called 'Fish and Cheeps'. George, who sat weeping, received the creature on his lap. But not even love could make it eat, and it soon died of starvation.

For five years two other, younger musicians, whose names were Mark and Steve, inhabited various rooms in the hotel, moving from better to worse or back again as their fortunes changed. Frequent

[53]

absences abroad were apt to deplete their funds. Then Steve turned more to painting but still sat in with Mark and other musicians, playing on his double bass. But Mark was single-minded about his music. He played drums, piano, saxophone and a variety of other instruments. After a visit to South America, in particular Bahia, he was inspired to base his music on chants.

From an early age he wanted to be a musician, but was a bad student, feeling certain blocks against 'school music'. Theory of music, he thought, was written by the tempered score. He preferred the sub-divisions of free jazz, the latest form in the evolution of music, best exemplified by musicians like Ornette Coleman, Charlie Hayden, Max Roach, Thelonius Monk, Don Cherry − with whom Mark performed − and others. He also played with Gil Evans, but found this jazz composer too electronic.

'Music is a physical thing − organic. Good music is a form of exorcism. Good spirits replace bad ones.'

From frequent trips to South America, in particular Brazil, Mark had absorbed sounds which he said still filled his ears: insect voices, the samba beat. From Africa and India, he recorded music for voodoo, cuca monkey noises, elephants and double cowbells, using xylophone and Moog.

Mark the Lark, as other musicians called him, offered his considered opinions while leaning on the railing outside the Chelsea entrance. He was always a little spaced-out. It was his great non-musical talent to know just how to score where grass was concerned. He was a connoisseur of marijuana; had sought it out in the countries of the world. He spoke in tongues when referring to the drug, reeling off the different names − Acapulco Gold, Panama Red, Moroccan Black − like poetry.

Mark made his first record for Capitol when he was sixteen. He also played in coffee houses. Now he felt almost ready to give something of importance to the world. It was the kind of self-endorsement the young require. Egotism usually comes later. But Mark, at that point, neither criticized nor tried to compete, believing everyone should find his own method. Ultimately he found himself a method, influenced rather too frequently by his favourite smoke which, like de Quincey's opium, wound through the corridors of his mind evoking sounds which he, the composer, heard more clearly and with more understanding than those of us who were listening.

[54]

Steve, a fellow voyager to far ports in search of the magic weed, also waxed furiously creative — after smoking. As a painter and an admirer of Jackson Pollock, he could spread canvas on the floor, fling paint at it and walk about on the top resulting in fascinating designs which were sometimes bought by Stanley and his friends in New Jersey. So intense was the mutual belief in themselves as artists that even though music and painting alike were cacophonous and apparently without purpose, insulting to ears and eyes, we onlookers and listeners would feel we were lacking something in ourselves through our inability to absorb the strange idioms. It was the drugs, of course. Unless one were also stoned the subtle inner meanings were lost, if there were any meanings. There may have been. But without meeting these new practitioners of art halfway in equal euphoria, one felt somehow left out.

As a wage-earner I saw little of the residents of the Chelsea when I first moved in. But in a gradual process the staff made me feel at home; and constant riding in the elevators, when they worked, brought me into contact with people who eventually became familiar to me. One of these was a tall, rather beautiful girl with long, fair hair and high cheekbones. She lived on the tenth floor in a huge studio and her name was Sandy Daley. The high cheekbones were the result of Cherokee blood and she came from South Dakota.

One day she asked me for a drink in El Quijote. With her was her lover, a young Englishman named Nicholas Quinnell with whom she shared the studio. Nicholas was in advertising. Sandy conjured up 'happenings'; these were the years when people indulged in a strange kind of spontaneity which was not really spontaneity at all, being carefully thought out and choreographed if it was to produce anything worthwhile.

Sandy was one of the best. Scuffling around on the fringes of the — to me — alien Pop Art world of New York, I found Sandy and her milieu fascinating. She 'knew everyone' and frequented Max's Kansas City, the hangout of all people who were 'with it'. Edie Sedgewick, Andy Warhol's superstar who lived at the Chelsea for long periods off and on, was one of Sandy's acquaintances — as were all the tinsel boys and girls who appeared to be sexually interchangeable and wore marvellous clothes that seemed less clothing than costume.

In all this glitter, Sandy moved with a kind of regal wisdom. Her happenings were definitely not on the level of raspberry jam smeared on cars, or people defecating in odd places, or the kind resulting in films like Warhol's. But as happenings they were nonetheless outré and unacceptable to those who had not been indoctrinated.

The year of my arrival, Sandy was working on an important happening with Patti Smith, who lived periodically at the hotel with Sam Shepard, the actor-playwright. Patti was small and dark and clad in rags. But they were special rags, hand-picked and of antique lace and yellowed lawn. Patti chose them with exquisite care, the same kind of care she gave her poetry.[1] Preparations for the happening forged ahead. Involved, besides Patti, was the photographer Robert Mapplethorpe, who was by then, as far as I could make out, taking the place of Sam Shepard. There was also a young doctor, himself a poet.

Sandy finished arrangements for her happening and called it, bizarrely, 'Robert Getting his Nipple Pierced'. A privileged few of us were invited to her studio to see the first 'performance'. There was a king-sized mattress on the floor and a couple of Warhol's big silver cushions floated near the ceiling. The room was dead white, furnished Japanese-style with a floor covered in white vinyl – a splendid example of what Chelsea inhabitants could do with their rooms if they chose to.

Patti, in her special rags, gave a witty running commentary of her love life while the young doctor inserted a gold ring into one of Robert Mapplethorpe's nipples. Robert, who has since become an outstanding photographer, must have suffered. We who were watching certainly suffered vicariously. All the while Sandy was busily filming.

The result was wholly satisfactory in the idiom of the day. Sandy was invited to show the video at the Museum of Modern Art and was not in the least disappointed – it was only natural – that a large percentage of her audience came from the Chelsea. We shared her success with pleasure and listened proudly as she gave a talk afterwards, standing at a lectern wearing a woollen cap as though just off a Dakota range.

Not long afterwards, and obviously because of the video's reception by the New York press, Sandy was asked to make a happening for the Coca-Cola Company in Tokyo. Payment was excellent. She bought

[1] The last time I saw Patti was in Edinburgh in the '70s while she was on tour with her hard-rock band, the Patti Smith Group. They were at the time very successful, especially with one song, 'Because the Night', jointly composed by Patti and Bruce Springsteen. During the concert, Patti's poetry was shown on big screens in the background.

[56]

her ticket, got her passport in order and awaited the final summons. It never came. The whole event was cancelled. We wept with her; got drunk with her in El Quijote. The cancellation was so typical of what an artist must go through, all the worse when success seemed so close. But then the life of an artist is 50% waiting and hoping. Call that 75%. Nearer the mark.

At about this time I had a happening of my own, although those involved would never have seen it thus. The incident took place at MGM in the elegant black glass tower on Fifty-Fifth Street and Sixth Avenue or, as it was unpopularly renamed, Avenue of the Americas. My office was on the twenty-seventh floor; the bosses — for it was a bosses' building, of course — worked and had their being higher up, the twenty-ninth floor housing such important personages as the president and vice-president. In fact, there was more than one vice-president. One of the most important executives with MGM at that time was named Seymour. I thought it amusing that the logo on his writing paper read 'Let the Lion Roar for Seymour'.

I had seen this man from a distance, but never spoken with him. He was tall, largely built and 'sharply' dressed in the latest cut of suiting. Then, one morning, I was summoned to his office. He was all affability, a true sales pitch projected in his well-practised manner. With obvious pride, he told me he had a son at college. This son, he said, was about to write an important term paper but, in view of certain complications which Seymour did not explain,, needed help. He leaned forward across his huge desk, throwing charm at me in a startlingly effusive way. They — whoever they were — had told him I was brainy. He liked women to be brainy. He liked them, I soon gathered, to be brainy so they could lend support to his son in time of need.

Details of the operation appeared even as I made mumbled protests as to my 'superior' brain. The son's term paper was a comparison of the poetry of William Carlos Williams and Wallace Stevens. If I could, or would (I knew I must, especially seeing steely eyes behind his glad-hand smile) write the comparison, Seymour would see to it that I was amply rewarded. My thoughts turned to money. Wishful thinking. My reward would be a lunch at one of New York's best restaurants (not specified) in the company of the VIP and one of France's most distinguished film directors, also not specified. I spoke French, didn't I? I did, unfortunately, since this led to my having to

[57]

read all the French material sent to the Story Department without any increase in salary. Trapped, I agreed to write the paper.

A few days later, feeling pleased with myself, I took the completed piece to Seymour's office. I had compared two poems which in their complex way spoke of death. Seymour took the manuscript and read for a moment in silence. Then he looked at me disapprovingly.

'What does concupiscent mean?'

The word came from a line in a Wallace Stevens poem: 'In kitchen cups concupiscent curds.'

I said it meant strong sexual desire. He seemed not to believe me and yelled to his secretary, 'Bring a dictionary!'

When she did, he read, frowned and dismissed me with less than warm thanks. It was the last I heard on the subject. When we met in the corridors or on the street he would either wave or, if close enough, lay a heavy arm across my shoulders. 'How's it going, babe?'

Perhaps I failed him, or rather, had his son failed due to me? I would never know. Later I heard that when his son was assigned an essay on Herman Melville, Seymour sent to Hollywood for the entire film of *Moby Dick* to be shown in the privacy of his living room. It is certain that the son enjoyed this far more than struggling through Wallace Stevens.

At about this time, I was involved with MGM's great film *2001: A Space Odyssey*, another kind of happening. The author, Arthur C. Clarke, had his suite at the Chelsea, which he kept for years, and Stanley Kubrick, the director, came and went, though the actual filming was being done in London behind closed doors. In reality there were rare occasions when my job with MGM, and its affiliations, did run parallel with Chelsea life. As theatre scout I met actors and producers, designers and musicians, some very successful. But it was the blind musician Moondog, a man I saw frequently, who was far and away the closest to someone we all thought of − possibly fatuously − as 'one of us'.

I first encountered Moondog in 1965. Tall, with long white hair and a white beard, clothed in red robes with sometimes a kind of Viking head-dress, he stood in all weathers against a wall halfway between our building and the Warwick Hotel which the Beatles had recently vacated. *New York Magazine* produced an article on him, stating that while his costume was 'his own business', his poetry was aimed at anyone who would buy it and so was his music.

[58]

Moondog was totally blind. Born in Kansas City as Louis Hardin, he had studied music as a young man and had lived in New York since the early 'Forties. He has been referred to as a 'primitive' and one of America's great originals. His poetry was simple — I bought some of the mimeographed sheets at ten cents each — his music impressive though conventional. The songs suggested Donovan and he made full use of canons and rounds.

When word came that Columbia Studios had persuaded him to record some of his 'symphonies', the reporter from *New York Magazine* feared that Moondog had yielded to commercialism.

'I couldn't have been more mistaken,' he wrote. 'Moondog's "big" music which he had been working on all his life along with his better-known folkish pieces, strengthened if anything my regard for his skill. He conducted the music himself — an awesome figure but a man who knew what he was doing.'

I often passed the time of day with Moondog and he was always courteous. He had his following and sometimes I would see a young girl offering him food or leading him by the hand. One day he disappeared from his corner, gone perhaps to the cabin he had built himself in Ithaca. Not long ago I heard that he had died.

One of the Chelseaites I made friends with was a young woman named Joyce Elbert whose second husband, John Hultberg, had taken such outraged exception to the interior design of El Quijote. One of the country's better painters, he was now married to Lynne Drexler, also a painter; and to entangle matters somewhat, they too lived at the Chelsea. Joyce was working for a paperback company when her second book *The Crazy Ladies* was accepted by New American Library for a $10,000 advance.

We celebrated. The hotel's sole stockbroker, Irving Baer, who seemed puzzled himself as to why he had chosen the Chelsea for his home, invited Joyce and me to his apartment for champagne. Irving's apartment filled us all with envy. It was beautifully furnished and his kitchen was a miracle of modern equipment with not a cockroach in sight. As the champagne went down, Joyce and I danced, she on the table where she sprained her ankle doing the Charleston to prove to Irving that she was able to perform a dance that belonged more properly to his youth.

Drinking was as much a part of the Chelsea as drugs. Excess was usual, and Joyce's ex-husband was a heavy participant, aided and abetted from time to time by Lynne. Once I accompanied her and John to the Payne-Whitney clinic and, as we drove along the East River, John's longish fair hair blowing, he leaned out the open window of the taxi shouting: 'That's *my* river. I've painted it all.'

Lynne was from the South with the charming accent of the Southerner and the equally charming manner of a Southern Lady. But she had a longshoreman's vocabulary which she hurled from gentle lips. Her hair was long and very blonde and she painted like an angel with a superb sense of colour. She could also sew and made me beautiful cushions from patchwork, the discards of friends' clothing. She made them to sell, and undoubtedly cheated herself. One day she gave me a big patchwork quilt like a collection of jewels, many colours, many fabrics. This was soon to be transformed, thanks to the clever fingers of a freckled-faced blonde girl named Nancy.

I didn't know at what point Nancy entered my life but it was at about the time of the Woodstock Rock Festival, which seemed to have been trauma on trauma, an unforgettable experience for those who attended it and for those who merely heard about it. Nancy was a groupie, albeit of a very superior kind. The object of her affections was Frank Zappa of the Mothers of Invention, a wild-eyed, talented, anarchic musician. Irish, forthright and with a wry sense of humour, Nancy literally fed the Mothers of Invention and would drop in at my office laden with shopping bags stuffed with food, on her way to alleviate the starving rock group who were staying at the Chelsea at the time.

This would not be the last time MGM was involved in a mild way with the Chelsea. The less tolerant members of staff still considered me peculiar for choosing to live among 'those weirdos'. At the same time there was a dilemma to be faced. They knew Arthur C. Clarke was not a weirdo, and *he* lived down there. Nancy they regarded as a typical hippie and stared disapprovingly when they passed the door to my office and saw her perched on my desk, overflowing bags from the supermarket at her feet.

My own feeling was that Nancy had been touched by the magic, or what she thought of as the magic, of the Chelsea, if only because it was the temporary home of many rock groups, in particular her adored Frank Zappa. When the moment came for me to ask her help, I was happy to know she felt that way.

The editor of *Show*, a glossy magazine owned by Huntington

Hartford, commissioned me to write an article. The pay would take care of my rent for three months, and I duly turned out a quite dreadful piece on another group called the Incredible String Band, of which my youngest son was a member. My reward, apart from a thousand dollars, was an invitation to one of Huntington Hartford's parties to promote the magazine. It was to be given at an extremely swank night spot called The Inn of the Clock near the United Nations Building. The whole affair seemed out of my league, and I had nothing, but nothing, to wear. Evening dress was naturally mandatory.

Nancy dropped in, saw the patchwork quilt and set to work. In less than two hours I had an evening skirt worthy of Bendel's best. Worn with a black, backless top, it more than served its purpose. That some of the stitches tended to come undone during the course of the evening enhanced its value to me; it had been sewn with love.

My escort Archie Carter, an impoverished playwright, had no dinner jacket, but got away with it by wearing a black overcoat with a white muffler at his throat. As we were met at the door and practically searched, I saw *Show*'s editor arrive wearing a paisley jump-suit. He was turned away.

Later (while trying not to hear Tiny Tim singing), I was accosted by my host. 'And who are you?' he demanded.

'Just one of your contributors,' I replied and smoothed the weakened seems of my lovely patchwork quilt.

I survived, by the effort of my friends. I even smelled good, generously sprayed from a bottle of Sortilège presented by Irving Baer. It paid off to have a token stockbroker in our midst. And an Irish groupie with clever fingers who was in love with the Mothers of Invention.

Looking back, it is hard to remember just when the flow of rock musicians began. We were passing from the acoustic to the electric era, but Bob Dylan, Tom Paxton, Joan Baez, Buffy St Marie, Donovan, the Incredible String Band and others equally valuable in their different ways, staunchly carried on the folk tradition. Poetry and rock music walked together: travelling troubadors in jeans, some splendid, others weak imitators. Bob Dylan composed songs at the Chelsea. A line from one of the lyrics goes: 'Stayin' up for days in the Chelsea Hotel, writin' "Sad-Eyed Lady of the Lowlands" for you.' One scarcely ever saw him; he worked hard and stayed in his room.

Leonard Cohen, one of the best known of the poet-musicians, was on

[61]

the other hand very visible. He adored girls and, as a consequence, easily lured them with his songs, beautiful in a haunting kind of way. He produced an album while at the Chelsea: 'New Skin for an Old Ceremony', in which there was a song: 'I remember you well/At the Chelsea Hotel.' Cohen's homage to Janis Joplin.

But the hard rock musicians were arriving daily and the building throbbed and thumped at various points. Jefferson Airplane moved in, Janis Joplin and her entourage; Big Brother and the Holding Company; Country Joe and the Fish, The Band; Jimi Hendrix, of course, Buddy Miles, the Allman Brothers; and Eire Apparent. These last borrowed my hair-dryer and went on tour with it, though astonishingly returned it before they went back to Ireland.

And still they came: Soft Machine; Cat Mother and the All-Night Newsboys; MC5; Quicksilver Messenger – a lovely name; Pacific Gas and Electric. Charlie, black lead singer of the last group, invited me to a recording session where I sat for too long behind glass, watching silent movements and mouthings as they perfected their music.

Pink Floyd came. One of these had been to school with my youngest son and a kind of rapport was established. When Nancy took off for the West Coast with the Chrome Cyrcus, a rock group from Oregon, she left her cat with the Pink Floyd. They looked after it faithfully then one day brought it to me, explaining that they were embarking on a macrobiotic diet and that this caused temporary loss of memory. The cat might suffer if they forgot to feed it. Furthermore, cats, they felt, could not be wholeheartedly vegetarian. I was forced to accept this explanation and took the cat to my room.

When she was not running down the fire escape and visiting other rooms, the cat was an amiable companion. My one complaint of her was that she ate the spines of my books. *Moby Dick* was her favourite. A notice appeared one morning on the bulletin board in the lobby: 'If anyone owns a pink cat that eats books please inform me.' I traced the cat to her reluctant host, then eventually found her a home with a manicurist living in the apartment house across the street from the Chelsea. This lady promptly cut the cat's claws before introducing elaborate injections and sexual fixtures, obvious prerequisites for city animals, according to her.

Cat Mother and the All-Night Newsboys were special favourites of the staff, but did not stay as long as Jefferson Airplane, who kept a hired limousine and chauffeur on hand, and were inspired to write 'The Third Week at the Chelsea'.

Buddy Miles was fat and shining. Quicksilver Messenger, one of them very tall and blond, stalked the halls behind Buffalo Springfield. Johnny Winters, albino, cross-eyed, friendly, carried his guitar in a white fur sling. Edgar, his brother, also albino, was often with him, and together they looked as if they had been caught in a fresh fall of snow. When Johnny fell victim to drugs, Edgar carried on in the strenuous hard rock tradition. Johnny was popular and there was regret, without criticism, for the artist who is forced through his own weakness into outer darkness. As Neil Young wrote: 'Every junkie's like the settin' sun.'

In 1968, my son Malcolm Le Maistre came over from England with his friend John Koumantarakis, known as Rakis. Eighteen years old, they had been dedicated flower children in London, castigated by the *News of the World* and the *People* as drug users, corrupt youth, and generally to be despised. They had danced in the streets with a group called The Exploding Galaxy, formed by a Filipino named David Medalla. They were both brilliant and unique, very much a product of the times. Now Malcolm had his own group called Stone Monkey, but only he and Rakis could afford the plane fare to New York, where they hoped to make their fortunes.

I met them at Kennedy Airport. Deep-dyed enemies of the 'fuzz' — Malcolm had danced all night with The Exploding Galaxy at Alexandra Palace in a happening/ballet called 'Fuzz Death' — they apparently felt the police would bust them immediately they alighted from the plane unless they camouflaged themselves as members of the Establishment. Instead, they looked like two handsome boys in fancy dress. Rakis wore a too-large pinstriped black suit with a double-breasted jacket. Malcolm had borrowed a tweed jacket, also too big, from his father. It had leather patches on the sleeves. With it he wore flapping, grey flannel baggy trousers.

As soon as they reached the Chelsea, they put their robes back on. Malcolm wore something voluminously white; Rakis was in pink. They were 'into' Eastern music and spent a lot of time in my room recording the sound of water, seated on the floor with a big bowl filled from the tap, splashing it melodiously. Malcolm was searching the hotel for a girl flautist, but could not find one, he said, who was not strung out on drugs. They finished the single on which they hoped to

[63]

project themselves towards fortune and took it up to my glass tower on Fifty-Fifth Street, squatting outside my door in their robes, looking beautiful and, of course, utterly strange to the rest of the staff, who from various floors in the building to peer curiously at my visitors. Hoping to see the head of the MGM record department, they eventually succeeded; but sadly he was not interested.

They did not stop there. A notice appeared on the bulletin board:

> Trans-Media Activators, Creators
> Sound/Light/Dance are Needed to
> EXPLODE . . . Exploiters of Mantric
> Sound structures, Chinese Ballet
> Quaki-Quali Akashic Records, Tantric
> Flesh-poems, Chakra Actuations
> And more and All
> Point Cosmic 0
> NOW   Contact
> Come See   STONE MONKEY
> Room 604
> Transcend
> Time/Space/Inertia/Inhibitions
> Masturbation/New York hang-ups

The note was well-timed. Robin Williamson and Mike Heron from the Incredible String Band, originally from Scotland and with a wide and devoted following, turned up at the Chelsea and read the notice. Room 604 received a visit, and from this began a long friendship. Robin and Malcolm collaborated with Malcolm and Rakis on a rock pantomime *U* which was performed first in London, then at the Fillmore East in Manhattan. *U* was the kind of show to make history during this booming period; but the producer, J.K. Hoffman, who had brought Stone Monkey over from England, decided they were too expensive a proposition to tour the US; so they were left behind after Hoffman gave both groups dinner at Max's Kansas City. With only their tickets back to England and their costumes, Stone Monkey, consisting of Malcolm, Rakis, Ishy, and John Schofield and Mal, came to see me. With the help of a desk clerk, Richard, who was on night-duty, I smuggled them into a vacant room where they all slept for a couple of nights, fed them and sadly saw them off.

[64]

Two years after that call for help on the Chelsea bulletin board, Malcolm became a full-time member of the Incredible String Band with whom he performed for five years until they broke up in 1975.

Before all that happened, Rakis and Malcolm prowled the city. They went to the Electric Circus to listen to a debate between Timothy Leary and Allen Ginsberg, returning to tell me that they preferred Ginsberg's philosophy because he was less phoney than Leary — Leary's advocacy seemed to go together with a taste for the martinis he was often seen holding in his interviews. Perhaps he was equally good at coping with both drugs and alcohol.

It was fashionable at the Chelsea during that time to attend the outpourings from those high on amphetamines. The young in residence seemed to think they were listening to words from the gods, as if the drug generating a rapid flow of non-sequiturs was not a drug but the source of infinite wisdom. I was invited to listen to one of these men on a Saturday afternoon, approached by two excited young friends. 'But you've got to hear this, Florrie. It's out of this world.' It was indeed that, but I could not join the enthusiasm. I had only recently broken myself of the amphetamine habit, formed when I was prescribed purple hearts. Possibly this drug took me through some very bad times, but at a cost. Under the influence, one is revved up to a point where decent sleep is impossible, one's appetite goes, with resulting emaciation, and ultimately there is some kind of unhappy climax where one either collapses or insults one's friends. The mind is occupied, at these times, by foreign troops.

The man in question, whom I was invited to hear, was slim and conventionally clad in a grey suit. I have never been certain that he was Timothy Leary because he was not introduced; but it seems likely, because of the awe in which his audience held him and a passing resemblance, that he was. I never saw him again. Ginsberg, on the other hand, lived at the Chelsea and was often around.

And still the musicians came, with their roll-call of ingenious names: Iggy Pop and the Stooges; Moby Grape and Mink Tattoo; the Electric Flag, the Loving Spoonful. And with them little groupies, lesser versions of Nancy. They sat at the feet of the hirsute performers, crowding the lobby or hanging around the entrance. Stanley Bard had exchanged the original heavy furniture for vinyl-covered slabs in black and red on which, inevitably, people lay as if dead, hands crossed over a daffodil. 'Knights in White Satin,' the title of a Moody Blues song,

[65]

always reminded me for some reason of Procul Harum, a group first made famous by its rock song 'A Whiter Shade of Pale', presumably based on the feelings of a rock singer performing while on an LSD trip. The reference to white satin contained a certain element of humour for me. When the building throbbed and sobbed and thudded with the music of dozens of groups, more rehearsal studio than hotel, Procul Harum entered my life in the quite fortuitous way which was the hallmark of Chelsea life. But it was not between satin sheets the young man slept that night. The bedding was pure Chelsea, worn cotton. I forget what the laundry marks were, but, knowing Chelsea sheets, they would have been characteristically from all over the city: Cornish Arms, Cartaret; Paradise; Holiday Inn; Americana, and so on. They might have even been original Chelsea sheets. The rest of Procul Harum had found spots on which to lay their heads, but one, the drummer, was left out, and in the packed house the situation called for an extra bed. At the time John Ransley, a well-bred Englishman who had turned up and found work at the Chelsea, was at the desk. Possibly recalling his dormitory days in one of the larger British public schools, he put it to me with the devious logic for which the English are noted (since the recipient cannot really gainsay it), that I should make up the extra bed in the large set of rooms my son was sharing with four other young people, including Nancy. The latter was away, and her bed was free, so to speak. In John's public school mind, it seemed logical that as Malcolm's mother I should make up a Procul Harum bed. Of course, I did. The others were in bed already, Rakis meditating beneath a sheet tented over his head. It was getting on for eleven p.m. and the maids had long been gone.

Years later, when Malcolm went on a shared tour with Procul Harum, he told the drummer of our association.

The Chrome Cyrcus, to whom Nancy had introduced me, had come from Oregon driving across the continent non-stop, spelling each other at the wheel. They were huge young men in cowboy boots and Stetson hats. Their reason for coming to New York was to play music composed for a rock ballet entitled 'Astarte' and performed by the Joffrey Ballet company. My favourite was Dick the keyboard man. It was he who also invited me to hear the Doors and Jim Morrison, who to our sorrow did not stay at the Chelsea. In the theatre, I stood only a few feet from Morrison, concealed by a pillar just off-stage. He was astounding. Dressed in black leather, quite drunk, beautiful

[66]

as to feature, he ripped out his songs against war, the Establishment and hypocrisy while his musicians extended what we all considered to be genius.

In that continuity of aberration which characterized both the Chelsea and, temperamentally, artists from different eras, I imagined that Thomas Wolfe might have liked Jim Morrison, who was often drunk, as was Wolfe; and they were both driven by the same demonic energy. Morrison's delivery, his hyperbole, his sexuality, were hypnotic, just as his music, on stage, was deafening. He and Wolfe might well have got drunk together in another time and another place. Janis Joplin might have joined them. Genius comes in different forms; but desperation is rarely mistakeable.

The Chrome Cyrcus also introduced me to marijuana, bringing it to my room one day and insisting I try it. They had discovered I owned copies of Mahler's First and Third Symphonies which I was able to play on Nancy's stereo, which she left with me while she went on her peregrinations. Stoned and listening to Mahler on earphones was, they told me, a profound experience. I puffed and inhaled and the world changed abruptly into an absurd place. Care fell away. I sat down on the threadbare Chelsea rug and it became an African veldt with grass a foot high and waving in the wind. I laughed, and everyone laughed with me. I found it a delightful experience, though subsequent experiences with the drug could never equal that first one. Perhaps I was not a sufficiently dedicated smoker. However, I never refused a joint when it was passed from hand to hand like a pipe of peace, feeling it was a form of protocol. Besides, I liked being pleasantly stoned, contemplating the iron fretwork of the Chelsea staircase where the pattern became a long line of dancing mannequins, each poised on an infinitely graceful big toe.

FIVE

THE SIXTIES – PAINTERS AND PUSHERS

THE arrival of the rock groups intensified the drug-taking which had always been part of the Chelsea ambiance. The corridors were filled with the acrid-sweet smell of grass, and acid (LSD) became popular. People 'dropped' it, some declaring they had wonderful trips, others just sitting with silent, cosmic tears rolling down their cheeks.

Serious drug addicts are a closed society, admitting outsiders only if exploitation is necessary. Probably only a handful of these same people would know about de Quincey and his opium-eating. But they would have automatically admitted him to the club. Exploitation was gentle, and sometimes involved a need for friendship. One addict in the Chelsea, a girl from a wealthy family, frequently tapped on my door.

'Florrie, have you any valium?'

She had to 'come down'. There was no valium, but there was coffee and talk. About that time my room, though I have no idea who first called it this – possibly Sandy Daley – became known as 'Checkpoint Charley'.

This same young addict wrote rather well when she had the time. She was also indulged by her family and had the first waterbed in the Chelsea. On holiday in London one summer, I wandered into the Paris Pullman, a cinema in South Kensington which no longer exists. The film was *A Bigger Splash*, a documentary about David Hockney, who stayed at the Chelsea. There was a scene in which Hockney was in bed at the hotel, talking about his life and Italy and Italian men. He was not alone. A girl was with him. As I listened to her, I suddenly recognized my young friend who had asked for valium. The lighting was dim; I could not make out whether they were reclining on the waterbed or not.

Inevitably, as drug requirements increased, the pushers arrived. Or artists, defeated in their own purpose and desperate for drugs, themselves became pushers. It was disconcerting and sad. One became familiar with the signs; hats or caps always worn because of itchy heads; sniffing, emaciation; a strange combination of elation and

[68]

despair in behaviour. Musicians turned junkies were a kind of anti-hero, and often took to dressing like rock stars and giving themselves odd names. One called himself Chanticleer; another, Charlemagne.

One kind of pusher was more dangerous. In 1969, a young black pusher named Angel shot and killed another pusher who was white. The latter died on the fourth floor in the corridor outside his room and the *Daily News* published a picture of his body as it lay on the marble floor with the caption: 'No Room to Hide'.

Inevitably too, the Mafia surfaced. And when this happened, the FBI were close behind. It was not uncommon to come home from work to find the lobby filled with tall, good-looking men in camel-hair coats and felt hats. We would be ordered to our rooms and told to stay there until an all-clear came. Alice Cooper, the rock star, wandered into the front line by mistake, his pet python about his shoulders. The FBI shouted; he fled; the python escaped, happily to be found later. To us, the FBI seemed slightly absurd in their uniformity, though obviously they were only doing their job. Perversely, I think we felt sympathy for the offenders, although a certain ambivalence persisted in the matter of the Mafia.

One afternoon I rode up in the elevator with an attractive young man who carried a big parcel wrapped in newspapers. He asked me, oddly, did I have a knife and did I like fish. Foolishly, I realize now, I said 'yes' to both questions. We went to my room where he introduced himself. I was momentarily appalled, as he turned out to be the son of one of the leading Mafia families in Manhattan. But he seemed charming and crouched on the floor untying his parcel, having explained, to my relief, that he had been deep-sea fishing and this was some of his catch.

I handed him the knife, he cut off a good portion and he asked if he could stay for dinner. While I cooked the fish, he went out for a bottle of wine. It was a pleasant evening until he asked me if I would like to take a ride with him down to the Village where he had some business. Warning bells rang, which I decided for the moment to ignore, even though he seemed nervous.

We took a taxi. On the way down he asked me if I would mind coming with him and waiting for a moment while he did an errand. The taxi stopped outside an ancient hotel which was due for demolition and which I knew housed derelicts and runaways. We went in. It was dreadful — long grey corridors, narrow and dark, with at intervals

[69]

metal doors more suitable for a prison. He found the door he wanted. We went in.

It was a tiny room, with a cot, a dim window, a bulb on the end of a wire, a sink and a young black man who greeted him as an old friend. On the cot lay a girl covered by a blanket. Her eyes were open but she did not speak. I took her to be high and knew it when, a moment later, my new friend went through the ceremony of shooting-up, accepting the glacine bag from the black guy. I wanted to get out, but knew I would have to wait for him to escort me from the hell-hole. I hoped he would be able. He was. Indeed, the shot buoyed him up to the extent that, in a taxi found uptown, he insisted we go to a bar somewhere, listen to jazz, drop in at Max's Kansas City. I declined. We had a few words, then he let me off in front of the hotel. After this, I felt I was a marked woman. All the myths of the Mafia came to mind. Since I had been with one of their sons, would I get preferential treatment? In the end I could only think: '*J'ai échappé bel!*' Indeed, that moment in the dingy hotel room left an indelible memory. It illustrated so well the squalor of addiction. The squalor and the greed. I wondered whatever happened to the girl on the cot. But, dammit, the fish had been excellent.

The younger residents of the Chelsea experimented with drugs more than the rest of us. But at parties everyone had a go. Knowing my tendency to over-react to feelings and situations, I attempted to make sure that LSD did not pass my lips. However, it did – twice. Luckily, the first time it had been mixed up in biscuits and had little effect. Next time, at a party given by Claude and Mary, someone put it in my drink. This time I found I could not walk very well. Lynne Drexler experienced the same thing. We left the party and made our way home – she was on my floor – partly on hands and knees. Next day, we exchanged stories. Fortunately, neither of us hallucinated. Or was it fortunate? Sometimes, I still feel I missed something.

Most Chelsea residents drank. Many both drank and used drugs. The underground film-maker Harry Smith was one. Harry had been working on a special project at the time of my arrival for four years. He said he needed two more years in order to complete the film. But he was desperately short of money, a fact we were all aware of due to his frequently mentioning it.

Harry was a smallish man who could have been any age between forty and sixty. He wore glasses and had long greyish hair tied back with a black ribbon, suggesting George Washington. His room was directly below mine on the seventh floor and he made lewd remarks about my bedsprings, pretending he could hear them. An impossible man, some people thought. A genius, thought others. He was something of both. For a number of years prior to coming to the Chelsea, he had dropped out of sight, living with the Seminole Indians under a series of different names.

We, who knew him well, were aware of the gentle side of Harry's nature, which he showed infrequently. Others more often found him loathsome, for he excelled in the insult and in vituperation. He was fond of the barb, the dart and the arrow, to say nothing of the slings. Usually his genius managed to surmount all this, until the insults went too deep. Harry was another who kept birds — budgerigars — and let them fly freely about his room.

One of the most shocking drug cases was that of Vincente Fernandez, who lived on the seventh floor towards the closing days of my Chelsea residence. On a night in October 1972, his body, apparently shot somewhere else and flung from a car, was found on the waterfront. There were five bullets in his head and body. The papers ignored the incident, though a TV news broadcast gave it passing notice.

Vincente was a waiter at O. Henry's restaurant in the Village. He was also a pusher, but in himself he was pleasant, flexible and intelligent and the nature of his death appalled his friends, those of us who used to sunbathe with him on Sundays on Tar Beach — the Chelsea roof. There was speculation and sorrow, followed by a period of hysteria. Vincente was dead; he was not dead. Detectives in tweed coats arrived and questioned a few people who, presumably, had been the last to see him. Stories varied as to why he was killed. The Mafia? Had he been muscling in? In the end his death, like every other, was accepted and a notice appeared on the hotel bulletin board saying there would be a memorial service for him at the Methodist Church in Washington Square.

There is little doubt that Vincente was Machiavellian and a perverter of the young. He was also, according to someone who knew him well, gentle. 'And he loved women.' He boasted more than he told the truth, yet at a Chelsea party when a newspaper man asked him what he did, Vincente said, 'I am a pimp.' This was the measure of his self-respect.

Decidedly he was a pimp when it came to Joy, a prostitute who took

[71]

up brief residence at the Chelsea until Stanley learned about her. Everyone was fascinated by Joy, especially when it was discovered she had had a sex change operation. She was often in El Quijote with Vincente. She wore long black, décolleté dresses; her skin was white and very smooth and her hair — probably a wig — was in a bouffant, piled-high arrangement and looked like fine, white gold. She moved as though she had no feet, only rollers. Suddenly she disappeared. Stanley had struck.

At Vincente's memorial service, which I did not attend but heard about later, there were three 'widows' present. But the real one of the trio, Vincente's wife, did not wear black. Bonnie Goldstein, the preacher, youngish and blonde, spoke a few words from the pulpit, and an unknown, long-haired man played bitter-sweet music on the organ. Another, arriving late, stoned and angry, muttered and moved about resentfully in his pew. Apart from the Chelsea contingent, a dozen or so, the other mourners were four waiters from the O. Henry restaurant where Vincente had worked. They all had very black hair and sideburns, and wore white jackets and during the thoughtful silence following the service, they kept asking one another, 'Where's-a-de-box?' No box, no body, no Vincente.

The widow had asked Mark and Steve to play at the service. They arrived an hour late. But the music was good, and no doubt Vincente would have liked it. Mark played saxophone, Steve the double bass, a friend, John, was on drums.

When Mark had finished playing, he found five bullets on the altar and wanted to call the police, until it was discovered that they had been placed there by a girl from the Chelsea named Cassandra in a gesture of misplaced romanticism. Five bullets. One bullet in the heart could have done it. One hand on Vincente's shoulder, and one last journey through the night. The end of a pusher.

The presence of drugs and pushers which brought undercover agents, 'narcs', to the area made it a common sight to see an arrest proceeding at the corner of Twenty-Third Street and Eighth Avenue. The prisoners would be facing the police car, legs spread, arms wide, being 'frisked' in the classic manner. The 'narcs' were, for us, figures of fun after a while. Though they dressed in a way the New York Police Department seemed to think suitable and in the manner of hippies, the effect of suede, fringed Davy Crockett jackets, wild shirts, beads and patched jeans was inevitably spoiled by highly polished

[72]

black shoes. Judging by *Hill Street Blues,* they do a better job these days.

One of these men invited me for coffee one day. At first I was uneasy and embarrassed. Then I thought, 'Why not?' Grist for my writer's mill. The narc was pleasant, well-mannered, attractive. He said he had never smoked grass and would like to try it in the company of a woman. Could I get him some? Any of my friends would have been suspicious, but to me the man seemed sincere. It never occurred to me, characteristically naïve, that the request was police-inspired and I was being used.

Not a regular smoker myself, except for the cigarettes which I had recently given up, I had to ask around for the marijuana. In due course I was given some and, as pre-arranged, the narc telephoned me one evening from the lobby. I had friends in my room and he ordered me to get rid of them. My uneasiness returned. The cop arrived, accepted the rather grubby joint I gave him and lit up, inhaling elaborately and looking satisfied. Then abruptly he paled, sweat broke out on his forehead and, to my horror, he fainted. I ran to the bathroom for a wet towel and mopped his face. He was not out long, and seemed humiliated by what had happened. After a few moments, he pulled himself together and departed. I never heard from him again and Sandy's accusation that I had risked the safety of my friends proved not to be true. It seemed to me the police knew everything they wanted to know about the sinful Chelsea and that my narc was as inexperienced as he said he was. Possibly the joint had been alloyed with something stronger than marijuana, a small strike against the Establishment.

The use of drugs at the Chelsea was, for the most part, a mild vice. Marijuana was preferred by the great majority. Anything stronger spelled nightmare. Heroin addicts are tragic, wasted and revolting. The needle, the abused veins, dirty bandages loosely wrapped and unravelling – memories like this kept me from attending Vincente's memorial service; though my good friend Juliette Hamelecourt, or Vicomtesse Hamelecourt, made a painting of it which she subsequently turned into an outstanding tapestry. Juliette believed and often reiterated her conviction, that drugs should be legalized 'to save our children' (she had three, all grown) which could have an element of truth in it. What you can't have you inevitably want.

Juliette was in my perhaps partisan view a great artist. Her apartment consisted of two biggish rooms, one of which was her studio, where at a long table she wove her stunning tapestries with the help of one or two assistants, depending on the state of her finances. She loved to cook — *haute cuisine*, which she had been aware of since her prosperous youth, and she had published four cookbooks and was at work on a fifth when I first met her, a book about chocolate.

Juliette's tapestries were in collections all over the world and from time to time she had shows, either one-man or with a group. She was one of the hardest-working artists in the Chelsea, and besides the chocolate cookbook she was working simultaneously on a huge tapestry (now on display at St Adrian's Church in Wygmoel-Louvain, Belgium). It was a life-sized depiction of the Twelve Apostles and the colours shimmered and the robes seemed to move. I loved looking at the finished and unfinished tapestries in the firelight.

Juliette had been born in Brussels, where she grew up in and around the court, acting at one time as lady-in-waiting to Queen Astrid. Educated in the Ursulines Convent in Greenwich, England and afterwards at Louvain University in Belgium, she was caught by the war in France and barely escaped, somewhere along the way meeting and marrying a man named Elkan. Juliette enjoyed reminiscing about her early life and I seem to remember something about her giving birth to a child on a billiard table, but I'm not sure; all of Juliette's stories had an ephemeral quality, threaded through, like her tapestries, with inspiration.

She had arrived in the United States in 1941 and became a citizen in 1949, having divorced Elkan after producing three children. Journalism was important in her life. She was woman's page editor of *Pour la Victoire* which was later incorporated with *France-Amerique*, New York's French-language weekly. Then in 1959 she was sent by UNESCO to Haiti as representative of the World Craft Council. She lived in Haiti until 1970, when she returned to New York to settle in the Chelsea.

Haiti was her love. She was fascinated by Haitian folklore and its designs and symbols and started a class to teach Haitian women to use these designs rather than the traditional ones inherited from their French teachers. This needlework was sold through a boutique belonging to Juliette. Her ten years in Haiti influenced her deeply. She believed in voodoo and witch doctors and hated the political regime of the time. The better to understand her environment, she took up ethnology: 'Whatever trace of paternalism I may have had,' she once said, 'quickly disappeared as I gradually understood the depth of involvement of the free African in his own world.'

[74]

And her teaching brought its rewards. She was always pleased when following the mountain paths to meet a woman, unknown to her, with a hibiscus from one of Juliette's tapestries embroidered on the front of her dress. When one or other of her thirty or more assistants had trouble understanding the design of a bougainvillaea or the twist of a turned down leaf, 'we took a walk in the garden and I taught them to see and to translate.'

For a time Juliette lived in Purchase, New York. Her culinary expertise had landed her the job of adviser to the Sara Lee food processor company, but she soon returned to embroidery.

A feminist, Juliette nevertheless believed in pleasing men. Her upbringing had taught her that. She was also devoted to her children, but liked to flirt and have lovers. 'I put perfume under my buttocks,' she declared in the tone of someone setting the proper example. This must have been an interesting fact for the staid inhabitants of Purchase. Juliette was more at home in the Chelsea.

Despite her terrifying war experiences and her escape by the underground railway in the Alpes Maritimes; despite hardship, fear, near-death, Juliette retained a charming quality which caused her to invent exquisite meals on the spur of the moment, set a perfect table, fling open the door to her guests with a delighted 'Voilà!' and an indication of the blazing log fire which she had lit at the last moment to give the best effect. When the chocolate cookbook was finished, she gave a launching party at which most of the guests, unusual for a Chelsea party, came from outside the Chelsea, friends and business associates from the other areas of her life. It was an evening for indigestion: champagne and chocolate. Pepe, her beloved, nondescript dog, benefitted as replete guests fed him unfinished biscuits.

My own evenings with Juliette were invaluable. She could haul me from momentary depression with a few words and I always left her feeling life was quite worth living after all.

Stella Waitzkin — she who protested in her coffin — shared Juliette's interest in witchcraft. But Stella's feelings were not based on ethnology so much as intuition. Stella had a haunting quality — trailing gowns and prophecy behind her. One of her original notions was to travel about the world burying glass-fibre eggs on former battlefields, beautiful individual sculptures from her studio that might or might not burst from the soil, like dragons' teeth, into armies of protest: another manifestation of her hatred of war.

[75]

Entering Stella's studio was like walking into a dream. It was dimly lit, yet glistening with the wonderful shapes she made of glass — pure and transparent or opaque and mysterious. Stella had wild springing hair and a gentle smile. She spoke in the same breath of witches and communists. If the moon was full, Stella's imagination bayed. I have on my mantelpiece a farewell gift from Stella, specially sculpted. It is a miniature blue glass book, the pages slightly open.

'Porn,' she said with a smile. 'For you, Florrie.'

One looks closely and sees the faint shape of male genitalia through the pale glass, suggestive yet real, like Stella herself.

There were other sculptors in the Chelsea but they did not noticeably fraternize, though I had conversations with them as rewarding as any. René Shapshak lived with his wife (who taught piano), but had an extra studio in a building along Twenty-Third Street. But the building caught fire and he lost his paintings as well as his sculpture. It was the kind of tragedy to make the rest of us wince, mourning the wasted work and the loss. There was Jonny (Eugenie) Gershoy too, Russian-born and easily given to emotion. She was a superb sculptress, a creator of airy, soaring papier-mâché figures, exquisitely painted mobiles, groups of people or single portraits. Of her work Jonny wrote: 'In my groups of mobile fantasies and in my "Portraits" as well, color is a vehicle of emotion, investing the structures with mood and light. In this manner, solid constructions are lifted into airy heights of special relationships, making a balance between the concern for purely visual sensation and personal and internal emotions.' She also sculpted in limestone, terra cotta and mahogany and her sculpture was exhibited all over the world or made part of private collections. For me, entering Jonny's apartment was a magical experience. The sun poured in, emphasizing the pure colours of her polychrome compositions, light sparkled and there was humour which could quickly alter with the demands of her nature to wondering gloom, but just as quickly change back again to laughter.

Painters were always more numerous. Brett Whiteley, a small man with a mass of curly blond hair like Harpo Marx, arrived from Australia with his family. They had a penthouse on the roof, one with a small garden and, lying on Tar Beach in the sun I used to hear the children talking to each other. 'A snail bit me; it had soft teeth.'

Barney Rubenstein was a dreamy young man with a passion for off-track betting. He painted racehorses and cars and trucks most beautifully and from time to time had an exhibition in an uptown studio, when he managed to sell a few paintings. The money would go back to the tracks and the horses. John Hultberg and Lynne Drexler came to the Chelsea from Honolulu in 1967. With them was Karel Appel, a Dutch painter. As their ship approached San Francisco, Appel, convinced it would please Americans, dressed up as Rembrandt, but was persuaded from appearing in his disguise before the ship finally docked. Mark Rothko lived and painted for a time at the Chelsea. And Willem de Kooning, another Chelsea resident, said of Rothko's exhibition at the Museum of Modern Art that it was 'like a house of many mansions'. Herbert Gentry had a mother who was a Cuban dancer, and ethnic difficulties had dogged his childhood, he said: 'America has lost so much talent through racism.' There was wonderful Bernard Childs and his wife Julia who had lived at the Chelsea for — now — eighteen years. And Toto, a French painter who had no English when he arrived. I taught him some, then along came a Japanese girl, also a painter, to undo the work, or possibly to finish it off.

Whenever we could, we attended our friends' exhibitions, enjoying the free wine and the uptown art lovers at *vernissages*. Pop Art was at its height when I first moved into the Chelsea and sometimes one looked wistfully at a print by Thomas Hart Benton of a wagon and horse crossing a field at dusk.

A refreshing change arrived in the person of Z.K. Olorantoba, a handsome young man from Nigeria. Z.K. painted on large canvases in a superb mixture of wonderful colours. He had a soft voice and gentle eyes. With his small beard and bright African turban there was something Venetian about him. When his exhibition opened at the Studio Museum in Harlem we were all invited.

Sidney Nolan and his attractive wife lived at the Chelsea and were busted by Connecticut police who found drugs in the Nolans' car. It was a common occurrence. Bernard Hailstone, a portrait painter from England, turned up, and studios being in short supply, he used a double-bed mattress board as a base, setting up his easel on the bed and painting away happily when he was not out seeking rich young beauties or fashion models. He was hugely successful, having painted Churchill and others, and later he painted the Queen. We became good friends and roamed New York at night, doing Scottish jigs on the brass plaque that said 'Proc-ors' (the 'T' was long missing).

[77]

Flower power waned, but while it was there it swept the Chelsea, inflaming the imaginations of those who came, saw and wanted to 'be with it'. Mayor Lindsay became hip by taking a walk through Greenwich Village with Richie Havens. Stockbrokers wore denim and beads. Hair was universally long. Among those who yearned to stroll among the flowers was a young New Zealand doctor who came to stay at the Chelsea. We became friendly and he talked to me of his innocent fantasy, longing to leave off his neat business suit and tie and replace this sober raiment with clothes which he seemed to think would release him from some kind of bondage. But, he said sadly, as a doctor he could not risk appearing trivial. I thought of some doctors I knew, but said nothing. Perhaps, he went on, a chain or even a few beads might not be too noticeable. I agreed.

When we next met – he asked me for 'a date', something I had almost forgotten about – he was indeed wearing beads and looked relaxed and happy. He took me to see *Oliver* and then to Jack Dempsey's restaurant for dinner.

I was pleased to dine in that particular spot. The last time I had seen Jack Dempsey was in Colorado Springs when I was ten years old. He had been riding an elephant. Dempsey was training there, and one of the leading citizens of the town, Spencer 'Spec' Penrose, had persuaded Dempsey to throw the first ball at the first polo match of the season, mounted on Tessie, a large but forlorn elephant who formed most of Penrose's zoo. The polo ponies stampeded and the match was delayed. Watching Dempsey, portly and prosperous, I wondered if he remembered that awful day.

Not all the occupants of the Chelsea identified with the hippie period. Indeed, some of them regarded the strange goings-on with horror. The centenarian Alpheus Cole, who had lived, it seemed, forever in the Chelsea, found everything quite insufferable, in particular the paintings in the lobby. He always advised his friends to hurry through and not look at the monstrous things on the wall.

I would sometimes drop in on Mr Cole and his wife, who had been a concert pianist. Their huge apartment was like something from an Edwardian past. Mrs Cole died, but her husband kept his grasp on life. He liked talking of his student days in Paris – he had come to the Chelsea in 1940 – and of poverty and painting on newspapers; of Millet, Daumier, Doré, of Poe and Victor Hugo. He had ground his own colours and remembered how in 1896 he and his companions had

[78]

celebrated the beauty of a particular nude model by daubing her with paint, throwing their hats in the air, shouting *'Chapeau! Chapeau!'* and singing in revolutionary tribute the Marseillaise. In 1971 Alpheus had an exhibition of his oil paintings and water colours at the gallery on Long Island. He was then ninety-four. At the time of writing he is still alive and at the Chelsea.

In spite of Alpheus's disapproval, flower power and the Pop Art scene continued until other, greater forces — the Vietnam war was one — brought them to an end. Indeed, Andy Warhol seemed to go on and on, but even he was not impregnable. Nor was his work. One sunny summer afternoon when some of us were gathered in Sandy's room with the windows open, listening to Elton John, Gregory Corso's little daughter kicked in one of Warhol's $10,000 helium-filled silver pillows. Another one floated out of the window. Then in 1968 Warhol himself was assaulted.

I was on speaking terms with Valerie Solanis, a rather drab girl who haunted the periphery of the hotel. She told me of her passionate wish to work with Andy Warhol in the same capacity as Edie Sedgwick and Viva, both superstars. Edie Sedgwick, contrary to Valerie, was delicately beautiful and floated through the corridors in see-through blouses and extravagantly short dresses, huge earrings and heavy black false eyelashes. Sometimes she wore leotards and a T-shirt or stockings with butterflies appliqued on them.

Viva (whose real name was Susan Hoffman) was beautiful, but more down-to-earth, and liked to talk of her efforts to make a garden wherever she lived. Now she lives in the Chelsea permanently, having survived the trials and triumphs of being a superstar. Two children with their mother's good looks have given new direction to her life.

Although I never knew Edie Sedgwick, I grew to know Viva well. When we first met she was living with a French film-maker, Michel Auter, with whom she had made a movie in the Bomarzo monster park in Italy. Edmund Wilson refers to this in his familiar acid way. He had been visiting the park and in one of his letters wrote: 'Someone at the Chelsea made an interminable film about it with Viva in the lead.'

The day she learned she was pregnant, I happened to be with Viva, and her anger gave her the strength to smash one of the pebbled-glass doors dividing the corridors. Then she changed completely, grew proud and happy.

'Let's have a drink, Florrie,' she said some months later. Then, in

El Quijote she stunned the waiters by opening her blouse and taking out one breast.

'Look at that beautiful, white blue-veined globe,' she said, then broke into laughter. All she was doing was nursing her baby.

Valerie Solanis presented a dark contrast to Viva in that she was curiously negative. It is difficult to remember her face. That she felt deeply I do not doubt, but there was a lingering, unhealthy trait to her, particularly in such things as her boast about her brainchild SCUM, or the Society for Cutting Up Men, and her passion to become one of Warhol's superstars was tinged with desperation.

One morning, George and I were shopping in the drugstore next to the Chelsea. There was a queue and Valerie was just in front of us. She became heavily jocular with George, asking him what he was buying, and if he was ill. George, equally without much finesse, replied that he had the clap.

'*We* call it applause,' said Valerie, with what could have been humour. It was hard to say.

Repeated visits to Andy Warhol's 'Factory', a loft at 33 Union Square, were unsuccessful for Valerie. Warhol wanted nothing of her, though she swore he had promised to give her a part in his next film. Mario Amaya, one of Warhol's entourage, has described what happened that day at the Factory, when he was also shot.

'It was a typical scene, people drifting in and out . . .' When he heard shots, he dropped to the ground. 'I heard Andy shout: "Oh, no! Oh, no! Valerie, oh, no!"' The next thing Amaya knew he was looking up from the ground to see a girl with a gun pointed straight at him. 'She was wearing trousers, a jacket, and her hair was down. Luckily, she was a bad aim and the bullet grazed my back, going in and out in a very freak way, and by a miracle it missed my spine by a millimetre . . . Paul Morrissey (Warhol's film director) was in the hall. He seemed very spaced out. "What's going on? What's going on?" He was absolutely ashen.' Valerie had shot Warhol, then run away.

Warhol was seriously wounded, but recovered; and Valerie gave herself up and was sent to prison and psychiatric care. When she was released, Stanley threw her out of the hotel and she came to me, begging me to intervene. I could do nothing. There were conflicting opinions about Warhol's shooting, publicity for which was over-shadowed, it was said, by the shooting around the same time of Robert Kennedy. Taylor Mead, one of Warhol's leading actors, is quoted as saying, 'Andy died when Valerie Solanis shot him. He's just somebody to have at your dinner table now. Charming, but he's the ghost of a genius. Just a ghost, a walking ghost.'

The next — and last — time I saw Valerie was in 1974. She had turned up in El Quijote and was soliciting every male in the bar, entreating them feverishly and saying she would turn a trick for only $25. It was terribly sad. I spoke to her, but she scarcely replied. She was shabby, unkempt, more desperate than ever. All the men turned her down, some with sneers, others uncomfortable. Considering Valerie's past fight for what she had considered to be militant feminism, this was the worst kind of defeat as she offered herself to what she had always called the enemy. This was the last time I saw her.

Edie Sedgwick, on the other hand, continued as Warhol's superstar, living at the Chelsea and frightening Stanley with her excursions into the extremity of drugs. One night she popped too many pills and fell asleep with a lighted cigarette, setting her room on fire. Two years later, in 1971, Edie finally killed herself with an overdose.

Patti Smith, hearing the news at the Chelsea, wrote a poem for her lost friend. 'When I finished it, it was like somebody could go to sleep.'

Edie may have set a tragic precedent. There were a number of overdose victims during the years I was at the Chelsea, but one suicide from drugs came after my departure. This was Sid Vicious of the English punk rock group, The Sex Pistols. An especially dreadful affair, it received wide media coverage. Vicious and his girl friend came to the Chelsea in 1978. Both were heroin addicts. Vicious killed Nancy with a knife she herself gave him, then the following year came back to the Chelsea and killed himself with an overdose. A recent letter to me from Alice Tibbetts says that a British film company has finished a picture on the benighted pair, likening them to a contemporary Romeo and Juliet for some reason. The film is entitled 'Sid and Nancy: Love Kills'. (After being premiered at the Cannes Film Festival, the film received excellent reviews, and has since become something of a cult success.)

The hippie days were gradually changing. We had all eaten soul food, hummed songs from Motown albums, enjoyed ourselves in a blackout which resulted in the best kind of conviviality where the entire hotel met in the lobby, paired off, lit candles, enjoyed walking in shifting light and shadow up the lovely shallow steps of the Chelsea stairway.

[81]

But Simon and Garfunkel were singing 'Look for America', and 'Be careful, his bowtie is a camera.'

A tall young poet I cared for went off to fight for Che Guevera and never came back. Activists were setting bombs. Malcolm X appeared. Black Panthers prowled. Angela Davis was a heroine and her sister came to stay at the Chelsea. We knew about it, and those of us who were interested spent evenings talking with her. The tenor of our regular lives, if there was any regularity, continued. A stockbroker moved into what had been Thomas Wolfe's dining room, taking the place of a strange man who had a habit of leaving headless dolls about the place. These decapitated forms would be found on the roof, cluttering up Tar Beach in a macabre way. This same man had a video of a baby being born and invited me in to see it. I hadn't expected what I saw and would have been impressed were it not for a certain aberration in his manner. Stockbroking seemed healthy after that.

Summers were still wonderful. We visited street fairs in the warm evenings, wandering through the Village for the festival of San Gennaro, buying Italian food and silly trinkets from stalls. But there was something in the air. From my window I liked to watch the *Leonardo da Vinci* come silently up the Hudson, set against a sunset sky the colour of the inside of an abalone shell. There were still liners in the 'Sixties, and several times we drunkenly saw friends off for Europe. Then, gradually, these stopped almost altogether. The once crowded waterfront was empty of the great passenger ships. Several eras were coming to an end.

SIX

A COMMUNITY OF FRIENDS

MY good friend Helen Johnson, professor of English and an historian, used to say we were a community of friends. We were also like a huge and not too selective commune. The pimps, the infrequent prostitutes; a limbo dancer named La Belle Christine who entertained us in her room; seamen; the occasional businessman like a sheep among wild horses; the dignified and distinguished, like Mildred Baker and Virgil or Arthur Miller; and the assorted rest of us — all living under the same roof with our anxieties, our collisions of mood, our general happiness. It worked; it all worked in that old building which was less a hotel than a pulse. Loneliness was a choice you made, and illness was always met co-operatively. No one starved. We lent one another small sums or cooked for each other. Sometimes help came from outside, but it always seemed to be someone who in his own way wished to be a part of our ambiance.

One winter I fell very ill with a strange form of flu — Asian, or something like it. Going to work every day, I had come to know one of the transit cops on the subway — a wretched, exhausting and danger-ous job. He was a Puerto Rican named Jim Rodriguez, very tall and strongly built with that form of skin disease where portions of the skin lose their pigmentation. We used to talk, and due to him I got interested in the curious graffiti of the subways, sprayed on the cars in what eventually became a form of counter-culture. Soul 1. Rome 150. Stitch 11. KY. Pollo 136. Mack 1-11. RAF i36.

Jim lived in an apartment house on Twenty-Fourth Street and was planning to marry soon. He rang me one day and heard from Ruth, or whoever was at the switchboard, that I was ill. It was the day before Christmas. Jim arrived with wine, bath salts, perfume, and assorted food. He stayed with me over an hour. When he got married, I went to the party and found I was the only person there — and that included the women — who was not from the police. It was like being accepted at a black party in Harlem.

Vietnam was upon us. My friends outside the Chelsea, those with sons of war age, sent them to Canada or paid their doctors to sign certificates stating they were 4-F (physically unfit for service) or homosexual. It was a fractured time. We at the Chelsea marched in protest with thousands of others, up Sixth Avenue to Central Park and a rally in Sheep Meadow. We noted that although the St Patrick Day Parade was permitted to use the whole width of Sixth Avenue, we dissenters, pinkos, bleeding hearts, were only allowed half the street.

Near Times Square we were menaced by tactical mounted police and their enormous horses. No more daffodils in their bridles, as there had been in earlier years when the flower children sang and had love-ins. Instead, terror as we were forced back against the wall of a building. I clung to George Kleinsinger's hand; he held someone else. We managed to keep our feet and marched on when the police fell back. From the windows of buildings lining the avenue, people leaned out to wave and cheer us on. There was no doubt whose side they were on. But the war went on.

There had already been, before this time, perceptible alterations in the Chelsea's atmosphere. The era of rock was ending; the drug scene was changing. Cocaine appeared. Cocaine then, as now, was for the rich, so did not become part of our lives in any way, except insofar as people liked to talk about it.

A favourite pastime at the Chelsea was sitting in the lobby with a friend or two, observing the passing parade. English visitors were always distinguishable: there was an arrogance about them. I remember Peter Brook and his entourage, walking fast as if they owned the place. A black retriever accompanied them. He was off the lead, which was taboo. I tossed it a bit of paper rolled up like a ball. It galloped off to fetch and carry. Mildred Baker walked by, straighter and more aristocratic than anyone.

'Not in the lobby, Florence,' she said.

And who comes there? Walking with grace, a flower in her hand. It is the Lady of Shallot, vertical, red hair theatrical against cream skin. But that is not a flower she carries. It is a vodka martini and it is Isabella Gardner Tate who approaches. A beautiful poet, author of 'West of Childhood', Isabella not only wrote, but lived poetry as well. She was in fact a poem, a rime royal, perhaps. She wore splendid capes and wide-brimmed hats; and made no secret of the fact that she was immensely rich. She had been married to, among others, Allen Tate, the poet. There was Rosie, her daughter, who also lived at the Chelsea

[84]

and produced a beautiful baby boy of whom everyone was fond. There was also Gil, one of the most popular bellmen next to Charles Brand. Gil was tall, handsome and red-haired – not usual in a black – and he and Isabella fell in love. She bore him off to Ojai in California where they lived happily together until Isabella decided to return to New York and the Chelsea. She came alone, but it was said she gave Gil a bar of his own to run.

Mildred Baker, a resident since the 'Forties, was a close friend of Isabella's. As assistant director of the Newark, New Jersey Museum, then a trustee, then a tireless committee-sitter on other museum panels, there was no humbug about Mildred. She was – and is – possessed of a clear, beautiful mind and was resolute at all times in her beliefs. At the same time she was capable of accepting any situation. When Tony Imperiale, a Newark Assemblyman, asked to be conducted through the Museum, Mildred Baker was there and managed to prevent Imperiale from closing down the Museum, which held one of the finest exhibits of Tibetan art – collected by Mildred – on the grounds that the exhibit was not quite the 'old junk' Imperiale seemed to think it was. Later the Philistine, ambitious Assemblyman appeared on television with Sam Miller, director of the Museum; politely, I heard, the make-up hand asked Imperiale to remove his gun and shoulder holster for the sake of avoiding misunderstandings by the programme's viewers of his attitude towards museums in general, and possibly Mr Miller in particular.

When Jake Baker died Mildred moved into another apartment which she occupies to this day. I missed my 'cousin from over the mountain' and have stayed close friends with Mildred ever since. Through the years she helped me often and with great understanding.

Isabella gave a party that was like one of her poems. A number of us embarked on Greek tragedy, reading the Gilbert Murray translations in Roderick Guyka's room, bickering a little as to who should read which part. When we attempted Plato both Roderick and Ed Callahan wanted to be Socrates. Roderick won.

A relative newcomer – this would be in my third year at the Chelsea – Roderick was what the French would surely call *un original*. There were varying theories about his origins – a Rumanian count, some said (one thought of Dracula) – but whatever the truth, Roderick was erudite and charming, Oxford-educated, a master of several languages. Though he read Greek, he loved the Spanish version of

[85]

popular comic books and would read them engrossedly when they came out. He was still living at the Chelsea when he died of a severe illness in the late 'Seventies.

Yevtushenko arrived, and he and his wife took a room on the eighth floor just down the corridor from me. A poet friend who lived in Larchmont read in the paper of Yevtushenko's presence in the city and appeared at my door early one morning, begging me to arrange a meeting. I said that would be unlikely, whereupon my friend rudely shot off down the corridor and hammered on the Russian's door. Mrs Yevtushenko opened it. She was amiable, unsurprised. Obviously she was used to this kind of adulation. But my friend was refused permission, though the refusal was courteous enough. Yevtushenko, it seemed, was in the bathtub.

I have mentioned one of my very good friends at the Chelsea, Dr Helen Johnson, black and brilliant and writing a definitive book on black theatre through the ages. This has grown into a monumental work. Helen is plump and quick, with a hearty great laugh. Invited to her apartment, crammed with files containing research from forty-one countries, I had the privilege on several occasions of meeting some of her friends. Names like Noble Sissle, John Bubbles, Kid Thompson, Eubie Blake: all very old, the last of the great early jazzmen. Eubie Blake played Helen's piano and I sat entranced. Like me, Helen worked a lot outside the hotel, teaching at York College in the City University of New York. She also wrote poetry. Helen lived quietly and it is possible few people understood just how distinguished she was, or is. Her scholarly achievements could fill sheets. Black theatre is possibly her greatest interest and to this end she established the Helen Armstead Johnson Foundation for Theater Research, aimed at unearthing historical documents, music memorabilia, original scores, arrangements, set designs, recordings and other data relating to the stage and to the Afro-American art of the theatre. All over the United States, people responded to Helen's requests for the Foundation. I myself saw the ceramic model of the dancing shoes belonging to Kid Thompson and John Bubbles which Helen kept in her room. Helen was increasingly vigilant to ensure the black influence in theatre was extolled.

Helen worked so hard that, although she was a very good cook (as I found out to my pleasure), she was often to be found eating deli-cacies at the El Quijote bar wearing one of her flowing floral caftans.

I would join her and we'd talk, I with a whisky, Helen with her bourbon. She has been described as 'a happy combination of a long-distance runner and a whirling dervish with an encyclopaedic mind'. But I think of her also telling me of her youth; her father was a chauffeur. It had been a long, hard struggle. For this reason Helen found some of the behaviour patterns of her Chelsea associates less than amusing. She was pragmatic and short of patience, but rarely failed to retain her sense of humour. Ginsberg, Corso, Harry Smith all pow-wowing in Harry's room, these and other less than impressed Helen, who might have agreed with Nietzsche when he wrote, 'Poets lie too much.' Her general aloofness seems to me in retrospect to have been justified. She was absorbed, dedicated and immensely hard-working, while most of the rest of us worked only when inspired, which was naturally not all the time.

Peggy Biderman was another very close friend, who would come through the door and stop to chat. She was probably one of the warmest people in the Chelsea, given to feeding the hungry, lending money, offering love. She had two teenaged daughters and a son who came and went, but although she had a job at the Museum of Modern Art for a time, Peggy seemed not to do very much. In that respect she was closer to the majority of us than to Helen. Yet she saw life as an artist sees life; and her vicarious enthusiasms had the stuff of reality.

In a biggish apartment at the Chelsea lived Sophia Delza and her husband, Cook. Sophia was a professional dancer who taught the art of exercise at the United Nations, the Actors' Studio and her own Carnegie Hall School. Her book *Body and Mind in Harmony – T'chi Ch'ian* was extremely popular as well as being amusingly written. Small and delicate, with an oriental look which probably had nothing to do with her many years spent in China, where she studied classic Chinese theatre, Sophia's speciality was the art of face-painting. It was always a joy to visit her. I think of her in shades of rose and gold, hair black and shining, a sense of drama and mysticism around her.

There were frequent impromptu dinner parties in El Quijote. Patti Smith and Gert Schiff, Sam Shepard, Peggy and I. So much good talk, so many fruitful ideas, a few of which came to something. There was always someone to breakfast with, or to eat 'brunch' with if it was a weekend. Some of us were invited to George Kleinsinger's studio to see Doris Chase's teaching films. Then there was a Post Office strike and George's shipment of 1000 crickets for the feeding and delectation of

[87]

his iguanas was delayed. He worried that his iguanas might starve and two musicians, Raoul and Stephanie, wrote a charming song to commemorate the coming tragedy. But the crickets eventually turned up, shrill from the horror of being incarcerated in the Post Office. They were soon incarcerated inside the remaining iguanas.

El Quijote was always a place to go, to sit over a drink and listen to the waiters. They talked importantly of this and that in colloquial English with Spanish accents that depreciated the importance of what they were saying. Manolo would surface, look around suspiciously, then in a burst of warmth buy one a drink because he felt expansive. Occasionally, if conversation waned, we would make up names for drinks. 'A Psycho Flip' or one 'Crime and Punishment'. (Make that double.) There was even a 'Far From the Madding Crowd' with soda. We thought ourselves witty.

Periodically, returning from the bar of El Quijote and stepping into the lobby one would stumble over a mass of TV cables and wonder what was going on this time. A German company shooting an 'artistic' film; a family from California named Loud who had persuaded one of the leading networks to pay them for recording their daily life. This was the Chelsea chapter. We were contemptuous, knowing we could never do such a thing ourselves. And not just because it was a betrayal of creativity: no, it was because we as artists were different from people like the Louds. We were aware of delicacy of feeling, the other side of which was arrogance, and the arrogance was a kind of self-defence. In the presence of business we yammered and blundered. When needing help, we asked diffidently and made a botch of it, chagrined that none of the better known organizations, Fulbright, Guggenheim or Ford, did not instantly bestow subsidies upon us.

But it seemed to us then, with the arrival of the Louds, that the arts were in a cruel recession. How could it be otherwise? And as the tide went out, we were left on the edge, beached and helpless. The Chelsea became even more a place of refuge among friends.

SEVEN

THE HARDER THEY FALL

FIRES, like the one started by Edie Sedgwick as a result of her narcotic carelessness, were common. It was during one of these that my friendship with the couturier Charles James properly began, though we had occasionally passed the time of day on the stairs.

Charles was a designer's designer, perhaps one of the leading dressmakers of the world. He was also an excellent painter and a man of great culture. Slight, dark, he looked Spanish but was, in fact, Anglo-American and English-educated — somewhat — at Harrow. His grandfather had coached Churchill for Sandhurst. Charles was to have trained at Consolidated Edison in Chicago; but he ran away to set up a hat shop on Oak Street and his parents disowned him. From then on he sought patronage of the wealthy or the successful. This was not too difficult to do, as Charles was undeniably a genius and in the world of fashion people acknowledged him immediately. Chanel was one of his friends; Balenciaga said he was probably the greatest couturier of the twentieth century; Christian Dior admitted that his New Look of the 'Fifties was inspired by Charles James's clothes. Charles sculpted his gowns and capes and coats. He was a great artist who refused to yield to commercialism, which placed him in a kind of wilderness. Yet those who placed him there still envied his genius. He made dresses for all the society women of his day, for actresses and opera singers.

In the 'Thirties, Cecil Beaton had photographed him and introduced him to the ladies at *Vogue*. In Paris, Proust had used him as a model for one of his characters. But when I knew him, he was fighting desperately, still refusing to compromise himself in the relentless flood of Seventh Avenue assembly lines.

Yet he invented the A-line and the wrap-around skirt. That he did not make a fortune from these inventions is all too obvious. Charles was an artist lost in a world of business. He simply could not settle for less than perfection, which always comes dear, no matter what the age.

The night of the fire, which was a bad one, I wandered down to his floor — the sixth — all of us having been ordered to leave our rooms.

[89]

The fire was contained within the wall of the room where it started, but took a long time to extinguish. In dressing-gowns or partly clothed, residents talked and wished El Quijote were open. Charles looked at me with a smile, then indicated an extremely handsome young fireman, saying that was for me. No, I said, the fireman was more his type. This made Charles laugh. He never bothered to conceal his bisexuality but, by a curious twist of behaviour, had married the wife of the man he later lived with. Her name was Nancy, she was beautiful, and they had had two children. Keith Cuerden, her ex-husband and Charles's friend, was a brilliant theatrical designer and helped Charles immensely in setting up shows and organizing his life generally. Keith would do anything for Charles. It was a bizarre situation.

When Charles left Nancy, Keith continued to buy presents for the children's Christmases or birthdays. I liked Keith very much and grieved to see him destroy himself bit by bit with alcohol. He was finally evicted from the Chelsea, but would return, unable to stay away from the person he loved most in the world. Often he was hospitalized and I would go to visit him, and when released, he would behave decorously for a time, but return to drink and schizophrenia. When he came to the Chelsea he would ask for me if Charles was not in. Once I came down to the lobby to find him sitting silently conducting Beethoven's Ninth Symphony − or so he said it was. He was dirty and in rags. I am saddened remembering. It is one thing to write about an artist's self-destruction but quite another to be around him and see him doing it.

Charles became my friend. He invited me to his room; it fascinated me. It was so untidy that the maids refused to clean it. The result was chaos and a kind of awful charm. Dusty memorabilia were everywhere. A Matisse drawing of a Charles James wrap-around blouse; the drawings of Antonio Lopez; photographs of Marlene Dietrich, Gypsy Rose Lee, Millicent Rogers, Ruth Ford, all wearing magnificent Charles James gowns. Nearby stood a dressmaker's dummy wearing whatever creation Charles happened to be working on at the moment. There was a dearth of chairs, so Charles usually reclined on his double bed, covered with books, drawings, half-eaten sandwiches, papers. An Afro wig was placed next to a mixture of fake orchids and real autumn leaves on the bedside table. On the over-flowing bookcase a ceramic hand held a zebra tail. Lolling by the bathroom door (where Charles would often forget to turn off his bathwater, much to the fury of

Mildred Baker, whose flat was directly below) was Sputnik, the gross, low-slung basset hound which Charles adored and took for daily walks along Twenty-Third Street, Sputnik dragging his master along in pursuit of some disgustingly edible morsel in the gutter.

We would drink brandy or Pernòd and Charles would talk of his youth and his past clients. At times he showed himself to be both bitter and lonely, regretting his current clientele whom he considered 'flatulently obese' and tastelessly rich. His thoughts would return wistfully to the past.

Charles was always writing off to various organizations, hoping for grants, or suggesting projects which he was sure the Ford Foundation would underwrite. But all this came to nothing, and I knew he was becoming penniless. One afternoon, he stopped me in the lobby to introduce me to an attractive young man. This was Halston, one of his students who had become extremely successful in the fashion world. Halston had agreed to help Charles put on a show at the Electric Circus – the former disco where Ginsberg and Leary had had their famous discussion – the proceeds going to the Art Students' League. Keith Cuerden did the choreography and designed the sets with Antonio Lopez.

Word went out. The jet set of Manhattan attended. Mrs William Buckley gave a cocktail party, subsequently transporting her guests to the Electric Circus by bus. It was an occasion of the utmost elegance. The affluent descending from their buses must have felt they were slumming in a delicious kind of way. Tickets were expensive, $26 for a single person, $40 for a couple. Students paid $10 if they could. I paid nothing, smuggled in shamefully by Charles. It was a memorable night.

Halston, as producer of the affair, provided the models, some of the most beautiful women in the country – or the world, since they were of different nationalities. There were eighty-five different designs created by Charles executed from 1929 through 1963 in London, Paris and New York. The models paraded in front of a motion-fresco of more than eighty enlargements of drawings by Antonio Lopez.

For a time, after it was all over, there was acclaim. Charles began working uptown in a studio which I visited once and which was provided by and shared with Halston. But soon difficulties began again. Charles had obviously taken over, and before long Halston declared it would not work. Charles went back to his old studio, where he occasionally taught students, and to his old fears.

[91]

My meetings with him continued to be erratic. When he discovered I had read many of his favourite writers, including Arthur Waley, he would engage me in long discussions on the staircase. Then notes began to appear in my mailbox written in Charles's strong, slanting hand. He preferred black ink and heavy felt pens, but sometimes used red ink. Frequently the letters were written on lined, yellow paper.

Mrs Florence Turner 8th floor corner ap't at right of elevator.

Dear Florence,

Someone gave me a box of this *supposedly* only man's soap and I thought you might like a cake since this weather one needs every sort of refreshment. Affectionately: Charles.
P.S. Did you say you did not know Ronald Firbank's books! If so their exquisite absurdity covering less satire than a mirror of society between 1905 and the mid-20s would also refresh you. Let me know about Firbank for I have some and all editions were always, and still are, rare.

Dearest Florence,

Thank you for adding to the greenery of my room; which will make the growing accumulation of unsorted (. . .) to be classified (one day) seem less like the effects of someone deceased who had at one time a career and a dream – a legend which those whose pretensions have wrecked the apparel industry have set out to destroy . . .

Frustration must have driven him to hold a show in my room one night. There was champagne and the model was Bani, an exceptionally lovely black girl who designed jewellery when she was not modelling. Originally Hazel MacKinley, Peggy Guggenheim's sister, was to have come. I had met her earlier and she had commanded my presence to show me a number of beautiful saris. They were her latest fancy and she tried them on one by one, but then flung them onto her bed in a welter of colour, seeming to lose interest. When I told Charles about the saris, he said they fitted into a theory he often presented to his students: that there were few original shapes or silhouettes – only a million variations. He also held that there was no truly American design, excepting blue jeans and work shirts.

Quite a few people came to the show but not Hazel MacKinley. Charles was tense, watching Bani anxiously as she paraded in one of his stunning gowns in white satin, at one point shouting at her, 'For God's sake, don't sit down!'

The last time I saw Bani was in the lobby. She had dropped some real diamonds, tiny ones and she and Burt Gore (who made jewellery) and I were down on our hands and knees looking for the precious small things.

Horribly, not long after this, Bani was found murdered in an apartment she had temporarily borrowed when its owner was away in Europe. She and George Kleinsinger had been close, and he was called to the morgue to identify the body. She had been strangled. I met George coming back from his dreadful visit. He was shattered and in tears. We held each other without speaking. The police never found out who committed the act, and some of us wondered if they had tried hard enough. After all, Bani was black, she had been murdered in the Village, and crime was rampant. We missed her badly.

It was events like Bani's death that made us realize, in our inner world as well as the outside world, that the winds of change were blowing.

Our dear friend Bob Gessner, the first person I knew at the Chelsea, died, and several of us attended his funeral. His sons read the tributes and we were all in tears. Afterwards we went to a nearby tavern and sat sharing memories of Bob. My clearest was of the graceful, curly-haired man who used to come by my studio at the MacDowell Colony on his bicycle, bringing a bottle of wine which we shared over our MacDowell picnic lunches.

Pasternak once wrote: 'Art is concerned not with man, but with the image of man. The image of man, as becomes apparent, is greater than man.' This was an observation that often returned to the forefront of my mind but sometimes it was hard to associate it with the people I knew, like Eliot the junkie running naked down the marble corridors, flowers in his hair, or Zoa haunting the floors like a ghost of the Vietnam veteran he was. The war was beginning to give America back its wounded by 1970, and the Chelsea took in its share of them.

John Berryman was another poet who lived off and on − and suffered − at the Chelsea during these times of change. His great friend, Robert Lowell, perhaps America's finest contemporary poet, wrote a poem about Berryman during his own stay:

[93]

... Brushbeard, the Victorians looked like you ...
last Christmas at the Chelsea where Dylan Thomas died

Berryman himself wrote to his former wife, Eileen Simpson, from the Chelsea and called her occasionally, though he was usually too drunk to function. Hospitalized at the end of 1970, he returned to the Chelsea from which he wrote he had been ashamed to contact her. Throughout 'twelve dreadful days at the damned old Chelsea' he had been in very bad shape, calling people in the middle of the night, and in general making so much trouble that he had 'alienated & alienated' all his New York friends. He signed the letter with 'Love & Shame', a parody of one of his own titles, 'Love & Fame'.

The 'damned old Chelsea', however, was his refuge just as it had always been for artists. Helen Johnson, like Juliette Hamelecourt, tackled the business and academic worlds with success, more than can be said for many of the rest of us. But the Chelsea, whatever its shortcomings as a forcing-ground for artistic achievement, was home.

Sometimes, when George Kleinsinger went off for an infrequent Caribbean holiday – it never lasted long because he loathed being away from the Chelsea – he would ask me to feed his animals. It was an enchanting experience once the boa constrictor, the monkeys and the largest iguanas had been removed to the zoo. The Tibetan bells over his door chimed as I went in, and the birds suddenly stopped singing, to begin again after I closed the door. The miniature waterfall tinkled. It was peaceful and sweet. I would play George's piano, then just sit listening. Save for the birds and the water, there was silence, not a hint of the fussy surge of city traffic; even sirens could not be heard. The room seemed to fill up with the Chelsea and with memories. Here we had mourned the death of Martin Luther King and Robert Kennedy; here too one could feel some of the past, not ghosts but a sense of emotions shared by people one had never even known.

George was very athletic. He swam daily in the YMCA pool across the street, and he played a lot of tennis. Sometimes I went along to watch, but only when he felt like using a local court in the grounds of the Episcopal Seminary across Ninth Avenue. The seminary grounds were an oasis for people – like George's own studio. A few students were to be seen occasionally, crossing the lawn where at intervals signs read in plain and Gothic lettering: 'Quiet. Grass resting.' Or, 'Please keep off. How would you like to be walked on?'

[94]

Walking down Twenty-Third Street, we were very aware of the street people. Winos with bottles of Ripple or Thunderbird sat on the steps of derelict brownstones. Puerto Ricans played chess on tables set up outside their shops. Behind a chain fence, teenagers, mostly black, played basketball, and down Eighth Avenue people were already going into the belly-dancing joints. Sometimes, after tennis, we would buy fruit at the stalls along Ninth Avenue, passing the VD Clinic (a place not unknown to some of us). Ninth Avenue had trees big enough to cast shade, and the clinic was set back from the street in a garden with even bigger trees. It looked like an elegant Paris townhouse in Passy.

The street people had their own closed society, penetrated only by the police when it became necessary to move them or to see they had proper shelter when the freezing weather arrived. But we at the Chelsea had our own special street person. This was Albert, brother of George the delicatessen man. Albert had been a prize-fighter and, although an alcoholic ruin, still showed remnants of muscular strength. Albert played games. He liked to form his hands into pistols and shoot it out with anyone he fancied a fight with. This was always done with the greatest good humour. He shot me once as I emerged from the subway. I was wearing a white fur hat and suddenly George jumped out from behind the newspaper kiosk, hands firing, and shouted, 'Bang! Bang! Snow White, you're dead.' Whenever the Con-Edison men were digging up the street with their jackhammers, destroying what peace remained on Twenty-Third Street, a full-scale running battle would develop between them and Albert. Although the noise almost never diminished when Albert attacked, somehow we all felt grateful. The Con-Edison men caught on, returning fire with fire, using their jackhammer like a machine gun. Albert always claimed victory.

When he reached a certain point of drunkenness and dilapidation, the police would take him off to the Salvation Army. He would be gone for some weeks, then would reappear, looking chastened and very clean. Then, gradually, the signs of collapse would begin again. His clothes were messy with spilt food and drink; his immaculate Salvation Army sneakers grew dirtier and dirtier, and one was lost. His socks disappeared. In time, so did he.

The police, in moments of emergency, impressed me greatly. I could not help but be familiar with the hostility they generated among my friends, and myself had no love for the forces of law and order. But New

York was brutal as well as beautiful. The police, especially the ones who roamed the city in their cars, saw things no human should be asked to see. They were certainly courageous, possibly in the face of great fear, which must have made them repress feelings by a show of none. And they were compassionate.

I was going down the Twenty-Third Street subway steps one Saturday afternoon on my way uptown. Mounting the steps towards me was an elderly couple. Suddenly the man gasped, plucked at his breast and sank to the steps. His wife stood immobile. I bent over the man and saw the life drain out of his face. A little stream of urine ran down the steps. His wife began to scream, and instantly faces peered down at us over the subway railings. But no one came down to help. The woman picked up the man's hat from where it had fallen on the steps and set it squarely on her own head.

'I'm the one who's sick,' she whined. 'I'm the one who needs the doctor. Not him. I'm the one.'

She had a middle-European accent. I called up to the prurient faces, asking someone to get a doctor, but no one moved. In desperation, I ran across the street to the Angry Squire and got Frank the proprietor to telephone the police. By the time I returned to the subway entrance, a prowl car was already there and two young policemen were squatting beside the fallen man. His wife had disappeared. The policemen were young and firm. One felt with careful fingers for a pulse in the man's neck, pulled at the skin around his eyes.

'He's dead.'

They asked me if he had been alone and I told them of the woman, apparently his wife. Where was she? I found her leaning against a big chain fence surrounding a building site. She was crying and the hat still sat on her head. I put my arms around her − but when one of the policemen approached, she suddenly stopped her tears and asked him brightly which precinct he came from. When he told her, she said that was hers too, and went off willingly with him to the ambulance that quickly carried the couple away, leaving the little crowd by the subway to ply me with questions. I tried not to listen and ran back down into the subway, thinking how that woman with her accent and her rakish hat has presented me with an image suggesting a prisoner at an insurmountable and impenetratable concentration camp fence.

Back in the hotel, life went on in its usual-unusual way. My good friend Bill Finn, a publisher, was asked by Stanley to leave because not only was he hideously in arrears with rent, but he also drank rather a lot. Bill was a beguiling man in the best Irish tradition, but he was also an example of the start of a recession, having recently lost his job at which, I had heard from others, he was outstanding.

To make certain of his departure, or perhaps because Stanley felt vaguely that he was honour-bound to retain Bill's personal belongings (though undoubtedly he would have preferred simply to hand them over on the understanding that Bill would never enter the Chelsea again), the door of his room was locked with Bill's belongings inside.

It was a Pyrrhic victory. In the room next to Bill's own was one of his drinking companions who, on Bill's orders, went to work excavating a hole in the wall between the two rooms. Luckily for them it was one of the latter-day walls, as opposed to original neo-Gothic. Like a huge mouse, the friend gnawed away with various instruments until a hole was made, big enough for entry. The friend removed Bill's belongings, among them many books, and put them in plastic bags. Choosing the right moments, he carried the bags out in twos and threes, and turned them over to Bill who, to my sorrow, took the sensible view, and did not come back to the Chelsea.

There then arrived Jim Lineberger, a film-maker and teacher from the Deep South and one of those small colleges with rural names belying the high level of their cultural attributes. Jim was supposed to be writing a film for Arthur Penn all about Nashville. His appearance was Nashville, as was his accent, but this belied a genuine artistic temperament. He had already written and published a rock musical based on the life of Joan of Arc. Jim was away most of the day, supposedly working on the Arthur Penn script. In fact, he was next door at the Off-Track Betting Office which had recently been legalized. A sad consequence of this addiction was that he frequently missed solemn script conferences at an uptown hotel, and forgot entirely about a cocktail party for Hollywood investors which had escaped his mind in the urgent pursuit of winnings. I began to feel his hold on the movie industry was weakening.

One afternoon, he banged on my door and when I opened it stood triumphant with a large paper bag in his arms. He said he had won $3000 and wanted to give me a present that would be of real significance. I thought of jewellery and was rehearsing self-deprecating thanks when he plonked the bag on my bed and asked me to open it. Inside were two bottles of Chivas Royal Salute whisky in velvet covers

[97]

of midnight blue and tied with golden cord. I was delighted, until he settled down to drink most of one of the bottles. Nevertheless, I kept the velvet covers, which for an unknown reason augmented in value so that I was able to sell them when pressed for cash several years later. If one of his reasons in giving me this present had been to remember him, he truly succeeded. The screenplay was, perhaps unsurprisingly, never completed.

Michael J. Pollard of *Bonnie and Clyde* moved in and he and Gregory Corso, bow-tie askew, could be seen deep in conversation. Shirley Clarke, the underground film-maker already famous for 'The Cool World' and 'The Connection' finished shooting 'The Portrait of Jason' about a black homosexual and his strange real-life world of cruising, celebrated with a big party, and began a new project. Indeed she was constantly working. In her autobiography, Anaïs Nin has written of Shirley: 'She had no money at all but wanted to go to India. She is a film maker. The *wish* was the orientation. When an offer came to make a film about French children for UNESCO she accepted and it led to her being asked to make a film on an Indian dancer. Her wish, for years, was the beacon. The probable and the improbable are only negative concepts we have to transcend, not accept.'

Harry Smith, the Chelsea's other radical film-maker was riding for a fall, we all felt. His general behaviour dropped a notch from impish to fiendish. He seemed hellbent on denying his better nature and went about insulting people, even employing deliberate racism by calling a black girl in El Quijote a 'nigger'. She properly broke a bottle on his head and had him thrown out. Yet he went on playing his Kurt Weill and Gilbert and Sullivan, making his movie – bits of which some of us had been privileged to see – and crooning to his budgies.

On my way out one Saturday, I encountered Harry in the lobby. He said he was going uptown to collect some film. Would I like to come? It seemed a good idea. He hailed a taxi and off we went. I was embarrassed, feeling defensive as the driver stared at Harry taking out a bottle wrapped in brown paper and swigging from it. I wanted to explain. This man looked like a wino but he was a genius. Unfortunately, he still looked like a wino. But there was largess in his over-generous tip. We collected the reels of film from a building where he was obviously well-known. People greeted him warmly, and I was pleased.

On the way back downtown, Harry suggested we drop in at Sardi's

[98]

for a drink. He finished off his bottle and put it away in the bag he carried, but not until after we had seated ourselves at the bar. Apparently here too they knew him. No one said anything about the pre-drink drink. Harry would not have cared anyway.

But he cared about his work. Jonas Mekas, another Chelsea resident, offered this description of Harry Smith in the *Village Voice*: 'For thirty years [he] worked on these movies (a one-man show at the New York Film Festival in 1966) secretly, like an alchemist, and he worked out his own formulas and mixtures to produce these fantastic images. You can watch them for pure colour enjoyment; you can watch them for motion – Harry Smith's films never stop moving; or you can watch them for hidden and symbolic meanings, alchemic signs. There are more levels to Harry Smith's work than in any other film animator I know. Animated cinema – all those Czechs and Poles and Yugoslavs and Pintoffs and Bosutovs and Hobleys are nothing but makers of cute cartoons. Harry Smith is the only serious film animator working today. His untitled work on alchemy and the creation of the world will remain one of the masterpieces of the animated cinema. But even his smaller works are marked by the same masterful and never-failing sense of movement – the most magic quality of Harry Smith's work.'

From what I saw of his work, the hyperbole was justified. Harry himself wrote that his work 'made me grey'. Detailed descriptions of the various films make marvellous reading and he sums them up, writing: 'For those who are interested in such things, Nos 1 to 5 were made under pot; No. 6 was schmeck (it made the sun shine) and ups; No. 7 with cocaine and ups; Nos 8 to 12 almost anything but mainly deprivation, and 13 with green pills from Max Jacobson, pink pills from Tim Leary, and vodka; No. 14 with vodka and Italian-Swiss white port.'

In the 'Sixties the Chelsea had been home to the writers of the musical *Hair*, Gerry Ragni and Jim Rado. Gerry's sister Irene, large and generous, had cooked for them as they worked. *Hair*'s opening – the dawning of Aquarius – and its success had given rise to rumour that Gerry, now rich, planned to buy the hotel: a rumour that had given way to more modest reality as Gerry and Jim simply jumped into a new and expensive sports car laden with camera equipment and drove away.

Now, in the early 'Seventies, Gerry was back with his new show, *Dude*. When the show unhappily failed he declined to discuss it with

[99]

commiserating friends encountered in the elevators. I can only think that it must have been a consolation not without an edge of irony that the Chelsea's dignified old halls still rumbled with rock music and people still sang 'Aquarius' in the halls.

The Manhattan air smelled of recession. Sometimes other musicians like Johnny Berger, out of work, would play and sing while waiting for the elevator to make its slow creaking advance upwards. Johnny eked out a living by playing in Central Park under the bridge or doing an occasional gig at Max's Kansas City, the Bitter End or Metro. Then he got a job in a night club, his first for a long time, and I sewed up his green, sequin-covered shirt for the occasion. It didn't last, but for these musicians there was always in sight, tantalizing, elusive, the hope of a contract. They never gave up hope.

In MGM people were increasingly uneasy as staff were cut. Even the huge bouquets of flowers, normally changed every day, vanished from the receptionists' desks. Someone stole an Oscar from the collection on the twenty-ninth floor. In the canteen queue, a man in front of me stuck a finger in the back of the man in front of him, who said, 'Take my life, I need my money for my old age.'

In winter great storms blew up, and watching them from my window I used to imagine they came all the way from Colorado, in the Rocky Mountains, picking up America on the way. Deep snow fell, and we sloshed and puffed white air like steam from the manhole covers and fell into drifts. 'It's colder than a witch's tit out there,' people would say and come back to report what the immense thermometer on the roof of the building of Fifty-Fifth Street and the Avenue of the Americas had to say. Foghorns sounded, mingling with the irritable urgency of police sirens. There were compensations, as ever. Bill Burgess, a large man of Scottish extraction, put on the kilt and took his beloved bagpipes to my room for a concert. The trouble was, his music was so loud and Gaelic and encompassing that the only way he could convey his haunting song was to be shut up in the bathroom where there was still a door of original Chelsea thickness. Through this we heard the sounds of the moors and the lochs and whatever we happened to feel at the moment.

There were signs of disintegration everywhere if one looked for them. But as much of it was on account of people's characters as on the worsening state of the economy.

Carol Bergé, a writer, started her (annual) stream of hate letters,

[100]

picking at random the targets of her venom. I received one. This was somewhat mysterious, since when one met Carol in the hall, she was chubbily friendly. In fact she was attractive and talented, but always in fear of losing the man in her life – who, possibly due to this fact, changed quite frequently. John Hultberg had a severe period of lying-down in Bellevue Hospital. Lynne, his wife, became hysterical and we in turn attended her in her rooms to prevent her expressed wishes of suicide being put into practice.

Late on Saturday nights, we bought our *Sunday Times* at the corner and staggered back knowing full well that only about a quarter of the paper would be truly read. When there was a lengthy strike and no papers were printed, the first edition after the strike weighed about twelve pounds. (Good for lining garbage bins – although the cockroaches knew no difference between the literary supplement or the business section.) Jonas Mekas, that shy Lithuanian, left each morning to write his column for the *Village Voice* – snow or no snow. When we couldn't venture into the night because of blizzards, or did not feel just yet like trying El Quijote, we would sit in the lobby and watch each other. Watch the ageing studs watching the women they slept with enviously watching the girls whom the ageing studs wished they could screw, and the ageing women watching the young men but pretending not to. It was all very sad – and very funny.

Then the summer came round again, and we gasped yet still sought the conviviality of Tar Beach, where we lay unclothed against a shallow roof-ridge in rows, drinking beer or icy martinis, talking endlessly and getting up from time to time to look at the beloved view of roofs and river, across to the Hudson and its ships and down through Greenwich Village to the very end of Manhattan. On a hot day a young man with a bare midriff and short shorts stopped Sandy and me by the elevator and kissed our hands elaborately. 'Chivalry is not dead,' he said. 'It's buried in Hoboken.'

Gradually, as months and years passed, the long-time residents who were not tucked away from sight out of *pudeur*, paranoia, old age or the need to work, were given labels, though these were never consciously stated. Mildred Baker was the First Lady; Virgil Thomson, the Grand Old Man; Viva, Mother Despite Herself; George, Purveyor of Joy; and I, to my annoyance, became Earth Mother. A former lawyer named Ed Callahan, who had dropped out to study his soul, deliberately gave me my title. I resented it, but could only be

[101]

grateful to Ed because he had at one time saved my existence. It happened in 1972.

The Internal Revenue Service was after me for $700 in back taxes — money which I did not have, nor saw myself finding. I was summoned to headquarters downtown, somewhere near Wall Street.

The first trip I went alone, riding in the subway with a black in a tweed jacket and a wild Afro hair style. There were only a few people in the car but he ignored the empty seats and came to sit beside me. Other riders hid behind their newspapers or moved further away. Drugs! was the word that hung like strip cartoon balloons over their heads. He's stoned, dangerous, to be avoided. I was frightened, especially when he kept asking me, his hands cocked like pistols, if I thought he should kill 'those mother-fuckers.' I said nervously it did not sound like a very good idea to me and prayed he would not take out a knife or grab me by the throat. In point of fact, he looked to be rather a pleasant man, though momentarily fierce. I wondered who had been so offensive that he was driven to thoughts of murder.

'You don't think I should kill those mother-fuckers?'

The passenger opposite me slid even further down behind his *Times*.

I repeated that I did not think it such a good idea and at this moment the train slowed for Fourteenth Street. The man beside me asked wildly where we were. I told him and he ran for the door, then turned back and to my horror made straight for me, kissed me hard and said, 'I love you, baby.'

The kiss had at least proved something. He was drunk. To avoid commiserating glances, explanation and 'I could have told you' conversation, I got off two stops early. There was a black cop at the head of the subway stairs and I surprised him by smiling as though he were my special friend.

The IRS people seemed not to believe me, and in a few days there came another summons, this time to appear in court. I was more frightened than I had been with the man in the subway. Consultation with Ed resulted in his agreeing to go to the court with me as my attorney. Given to wearing T-shirts, patched jeans and sneakers, Ed still had one suit which he put on and we set off for the judiciary.

The entire episode was like another Chelsea happening. First of all, we had to sit waiting on a hard bench while the clerk of the court made irritated efforts to fix his broken recording machine. Eventually, I made my statement and we were called into the judge's chambers. The judge was young and friendly. He seemed charmed to learn that we both lived in the notorious Chelsea Hotel and asked us what we did. Ed said he was studying Eastern religion, or something of the sort; I said I was a writer. The judge sighed. Ah, how wonderful. He himself had always wanted to do a thesis on Chaucer, whom he adored. We talked about Chaucer. The judge asked more questions. He had read my papers; he knew my circumstances and abruptly he said I was free to go. Case dismissed.

Earth Mother and the Eastern mystic went to the nearest bar.

Ed Callahan acquired a dog which, still identifying with the Classics, he named Demeter. The dog did not seem to mind. But Ed went off for a holiday — God knows how he paid for it, but one did not inquire — and asked me to look after Demeter. Remembering his kindness to me over the income tax affair, I agreed. Demeter was thin and nervous, with more than a trace of greyhound in her. I took her for walks early in the morning, a novel experience. There was no traffic; the streets — it was summer — were still fresh and clean from the water-wagon's recent passage. No one was about, save the odd drunk who, certain of safety and convinced he was sober, wavered down the middle of the street only to cant hastily towards the gutter if a car bleated angrily. The drunks gave the impression of dogged certainty in their sense of direction, imagining they walked a straight line — the shortest distance between two points, sobriety and inebriation.

Drunks who remained seated could be just as much of a nuisance. A large German named Peter Rheiner took up residence around this time. He had a curious calling. He 'hunted' wild animals in Africa to sell to zoos throughout the world, shooting them with tranquillizers. He drank a great deal and when in his cups became insultingly argumentative, fixing you with pale blue eyes and waving his glass. I once made the mistake of mentioning Joy Adamson to him. (Joy Adamson had been at the MacDowell Colony during my first stay, and my memories of her are not unmitigated pleasure. Discovering that I worked for MGM, she had demanded in her Teutonic way that I help her with the movie script she was writing of *Born Free*, which I had declined politely to do, pointing out that I too was writing a book.) Peter then embarked on a tirade about those who set animals free to fend for themselves after bringing them up in captivity. I wanted to say that, for my part, I felt it was not the same kind of

[103]

captivity as a zoo, but with Peter's capacity for alcohol-driven abuse, I kept my mouth shut.

On a certain day in the early 'Seventies another Carol appeared in our midst, to be followed nine months later by Carol's baby. That really should read CAROL'S BABY. She was a headline, a baby in capitals: her name was Francesca and we all gave birth to her.

Carol was tall, dark, rather beautiful in a gypsy way. She was Mother Courage on the Steppes; she was a bedraggled, slightly super-annuated hippie on other occasions. She was also a trifle mad and was rapidly driving Stanley to the same condition.

Carol's lover was Francis, a tall, diffident young man who suggested a tree partially cut down with moss and vines growing from the crannies. He always wore a drooping wool cap and glasses. Fearing cats, he slept with his glasses on in case a cat should walk across his face. While Francis was at the Chelsea, a cat was hurled down the stairwell. I think it survived, and the two events may have been coincidental. Carol adored Francis, and stuffed him with a surfeit of pure, whole food. Vegetarianism with Carol was a religion – as was the pregnancy which soon became visible.

However, doubt broke in. 'Shall I, or shall I not, have an abortion?' she asked me, once more dragged into the role of Earth Mother. But the doubts and the pregnancy continued until it was too late to consider abortion. Carol trailed through the lobby in long, dusty ruffles and bare feet. Francis was evicted for non-payment of rent, but Stanley, showing compassion, allowed Carol to stay until the baby was born.

The day arrived. Mark, the musician, asked me to be a kind of midwife, a position I dreaded. (Carol was using Mark's room from time to time, being unable to pay for her own.) Then, at the last moment, middle-class upbringing prevailed and Carol went off to hospital, returning almost immediately and almost certainly prema-turely since the baby had been a 'blue' baby requiring blood trans-fusions.

Francesca, with doting parents, made a triumphant re-entry to the Chelsea just as if they were paid-up royalty. Stanley let them stay in one of the rooms on the second floor, the kind reserved for itinerants of the low-paying type. We all went to see Francesca. She was tiny and almost invisible in a variety of odd shawls. There was no cradle, no bath, no baby paraphernalia. Carol had put her in a bureau drawer and placed a lit candle at each end. All this was too much for the management, and at this point it became clear that Carol's departure was desperately needed. She had no money, she resisted all efforts to send medical help or even a visiting nurse. Finally the police were called and Carol was arrested, screaming and fighting and throwing garbage at the men in blue – a passionate gypsy, in full madness. The police withdrew, saying other methods must be found to remove her, especially with the child.

Carol was unperturbed, but again free of the law. 'At what age do their eyes change colour?' she asked me, the all-knowing because I had had three children of my own. 'Maybe I should just say "nuts" to Dr Spock. When I needed him he was not political.' This remark puzzled me no less than a lot of Carol's remarks. She was offered $100 to leave. She refused. Again the police were summoned. Carol rounded on Stanley. 'You must be nice to me, Stanley, so I can like you. If I don't like you I can't pay you.'

The truth was that Carol had a wealthy family; was, in fact, the owner of a considerable acreage somewhere in the South; but Stanley had given up. 'Forget what you owe us, Carol. Just go,' he said. She did not go immediately, but was in the end defeated.

The little black rabbit she had bought for Francesca before the child was ever born, and which ran around whichever room Carol happened to be living in, leaving a trail of droppings, was given away. From being a darling it became 'too dirty', and a puppy was found to take its place. After a time Carol simply departed with puppy, baby and forty-four shopping bags, to take up residence in a two-room apartment in the old Ansonia uptown, where the puppy began to defecate regularly on the polished floor. Ed Callahan was summoned to remove the dog, only to be confronted by the problem of a puppy versus Ed's six angry cats (which had replaced Demeter the dog). Carol visited daily to make sure the puppy was well cared for.

Her stay at the Ansonia did not last long. Evicted, she stormed down to see us, saying she had been 'betrayed' by the marshalls: 'They didn't even say they were coming to see me.' They had taken all her furniture, leaving her with a naked baby – she said – and her shopping bags, in which 'there were these little insects.' Cockroaches, of course.

There was at the time a recent Vietnam veteran staying at the Chelsea. I cannot now remember why he had been allowed to quit the army, but in some way he had been declared 4-F. He wanted to be a writer, but had used all his veteran's pay on a taxi medallion.[1] Who better than to help Carol move out of the Ansonia – for nothing, of course, if she had her way. Eric was a gentle soul. It seemed unlikely to look at him that he had faced the horrors in South-East Asia. He had a girl named Claire whom he sent for from the Midwestern state where both had been born. She was sixteen and a half, plump as a partridge and very pretty. Without hesitation she took a job as a stripper in a joint off Times Square. She seemed to enjoy herself in the role, and earned a lot of money. Eric confessed he did not like it, but they were never behind with their rent.

Loading baby and bags into his cab, Eric drove Carol to the International Hotel at Kennedy Airport. The hotel would not receive her, but by then Eric had departed to make his rounds. He returned to find her outside the hotel. She had hailed another taxi and driven around looking all through the airport for Pampers and diapers. The taxi driver, apparently moved by this show of maternity, allowed her to spend the night at his place, platonically and with some bewilderment.

It was the last we heard of Carol for a year. She returned on Francesca's first birthday in a huge school bus painted red and with a notice announcing that, to celebrate the occasion, there would be a picnic. The bus would leave the Chelsea on Saturday around noon. There was a huge photograph of Francesca and many balloons. We all paid a visit to Carol, Francis and Francesca. The bus was elaborately fitted out and we assumed Carol had realized some of the money she talked about but never seemed to have. Francesca looked well enough. I remembered what Juliette Hamelecourt had said to me when I worried about the baby's health. Just wait and see; she would survive despite the lack of routine and the casual conveyance from place to place. Apparently Juliette had been right. Yet I sometimes wonder about Francesca.

Stella returned from burying eggs, and I dropped into Room 403. She was in a talkative mood. I was interested to learn she had studied to be an actress between the ages of sixteen and twenty-one. 'But I really see myself as a chestnut vendor in Delancey Street. Imagine a girl in a leather jacket like Amelia Earhart.' I contemplated a row of glass encyclopaedias – one of Stella's commissions – and wondered

[1] A New York taxi medallion costs around $3000. It is the guarantee for the driver, showing that he is independent and the sole owner. To own a medallion is to be one of the elite.

what she meant by being a chestnut vendor. Did it matter what she meant? The whole point of the Chelsea, it seemed to me, and our reason for loving it, was that we accepted without questioning. Even Carol's histrionics. A notice that appeared anonymously on the bulletin board about this time seemed in some obscure way to confirm that this attitude was the correct one: 'Prejudice is being down on what you are not up on.'

This could also have applied in a small way to the hideously pointless war in Vietnam. When the head of the Vietnam Veterans Association moved into the Chelsea, we knew our protest marches could not help when it came to individuals, because he had left his legs behind on the battle field and now rolled through the Chelsea corridors in a wheelchair. But he worked tirelessly and he organized the Vietnam Veterans' March up Sixth Avenue, leading it in his paraplegic chair. Two film-makers at the Chelsea were there to record the march — Frank and Laura Cavesanti — and the resulting video was shown at the Museum of Modern Art. Once again, as we had done before with Sandy's film, we all went to see it. But this kind of happening was for real. Some of us came away in tears.

EIGHT

LOVE IN A CHANGING CLIMATE

ALWAYS there was love and sex at the Chelsea. As Virgil Thomson said, they were there if you wanted them. And people did. All kinds of sex and love, the two often synonymous and always available. Romantic love, romantic lust, lust and love, thriving in whatever form it comes: as a gift to a lonely friend, just between men and women, boys and men, girls and women, girls and girls, women and boys, girls and men. It was there throbbing away, keeping the creative bloodstream flowing. Commercial love existed too, though it was never visible, stemming from the squalid phone call from the lobby, a surreptitious visitor, unknown in the elevator.

The bulletin board frequently offered love in the form of telephone numbers, or just simple goodbyes, like the one from a Dutch artist, Louwrien, who left the following note before she returned to Amsterdam: 'Bye, Mark. Bye, Steve. Bye, Gregory. Bye, George and Doris. Bye, Neil and Christine, Carol and Lois. Bye, Florence. Bye, Peggy. Bye, Stella. But our goodbye is never forever. Love, Louwrien, Nov. 18, 1972.' While in New York, Louwrien had appeared on television to tell the world about her theory of sex. It should always be two women and one man, she maintained. She herself lived that way and found it ideal.

It was not uncommon to meet a friend in the corridor looking shining and newly minted, telling you unaffectedly that he — it was usually a 'he', perhaps men felt the urge to spell out their contentment more than did women, or perhaps they were more easily contented — had just had 'the most marvellous sex'.

We all had sexual partners or exchanged partners or fell in love, involving ourselves happily in this sometimes desperate but most important aspect of human experience.

Edna St Vincent Millay wrote nostalgically about love: 'What lips my lips have kissed and where and why/ I have forgotten, and what arms have lain/Under my head till morning; but the rain/Is full of ghosts tonight, that tap and sigh/Upon the glass and listen for reply,/

And in my heart there stirs a quiet pain/For unremembered lads that not again/Will turn to me at midnight with a cry'.

I gave considerable thought to this poem – it sounds so pretty, so delicately romantic. But could she not have short-changed herself, hidden what really happens behind a scrim that might just as well be lace-trimmed like Barbara Cartland? Not that one should dwell on the farts and warts and snores of a relationship, although semen on the sheets is always important.

And those forgotten lads. Perhaps she never really cared for them at all, and turned them into ghosts because it was more convenient and makes better material for a poem. She was right though about the pain. There's always pain; and one cannot forget as easily as she does. There are a million things to remember in love.

Why not start with clothes, moving from the intricate buttons (or do they have zips today?) of salacious sailors to tweeds and recognizable jackets and shirts with button-down collars to the casual parade of hip garments, fringe and glimmer from metal buckles and studs, strange colours, and the shiny, seamless stiff dress of substitute cloths, often zipless, sticking until pulled hard apart with a rip like eructation: the clothing of technology. Shaggy sweaters and chino pants, socks to be thrown away. And boots. What a loss never to have heard that splendid, anticipatory double thud of boots falling or being kicked off, one after the other.

The most coveted arrangement was a twosome, a little marriage with the couple sharing one apartment. This had the mark of permanence although, heaven knows, permanence could be quickly dissipated by jealousy, sexual greed, competition. George Kleinsinger adored women, but preferred the one-and-one relationship; he even married his partners. More often, sex was diffuse. The main thing was to recognize it and indulge in familiarity. There was a lot of loneliness at the Chelsea and the usual mistake was made about one-night stands being the antidote for opening the door of one's room, knowing no one would be waiting.

There resulted a certain feverish pursuit on the part of both sexes. Work and strange hours covering plays in or out of New York kept me in a reasonable state which was not exactly sexual poverty, and being older than some of my friends, I did not expect too much.

Nevertheless, this was to change. In 1969 John Ransley, the afore-mentioned night clerk distinguished by the fact that he had been

[109]

to an English public school, introduced me to one of his newest friends – he had probably found him wandering about the New York Bus Terminal wondering where to go for the night, and taken him back for a meal. His name was Roy Haas and he came from the Deep South somewhere. Around six feet three or four, he was very thin but with an unconscious grace. I marvelled at his beauty and turned myself and my thoughts away from his youth – he was only twenty-two years old – with his limpid dark eyes and eyelashes like a child's. His mouth was sculptured and, because of the thinness of his face, seemed especially sensual. His hair was dark. He sat on John's bed playing an acoustic guitar abominably, and singing a duet with Bani (this was before she met such a terrible end), who obviously also found him overwhelming.

That was the first, and I presumed it to be the last, time I saw him. Then New Year's Eve came that year without plan or person in my life. It was like the worst Sunday one could ever spend, lengthening as the night approached without hope or anticipation.

What to do? I tried not to think of my family far across the ocean. I tried to resist the need for conviviality which the New Year's advent induced. George worried about me, but had his own plans. Most years, I had been invited to parties. Not this year. I walked around the corner to the Angry Squire and ordered a steak and a lot of drinks.

As I was eating, listening to the juke box, getting a little drunk, I noticed a tall young man who kept walking by, glancing at me as he passed. Then I recognized him. Roy Haas. The third or fourth trip he paused and said 'hello'. The next time he asked if he could sit down. I said 'yes'. So it began. He came back with me and stayed for six months. No one made comment; everyone seemed pleased for me. I think they knew love when they saw it.

'I sure like your little husband,' said Irene, the maid on our floor.

'*Quelle beauté!*' said Jonny Gershoy riding with us in the elevator, and invited us up to her penthouse for tea. Roy sat entranced by the colour of her mobiles and figures.

A country bumpkin, barely literate, but with the soul of a true, unrealized artist, Roy fitted well in the Chelsea ambiance. He adored George Kleinsinger and wanted to be his bodyguard, which made us laugh since George was the last person to want or need a bodyguard.

When the Exploding Galaxy arrived to perform at the Fillmore East with the Incredible String Band, Roy came with me, together with a number of other friends from the Chelsea. The Pink Floyd were also

[110]

there, sitting just in front of us, loyally clapping through the disapproval of an audience who had come to hear the Incredible String Band, not the Exploding Galaxy. People began walking out. 'I thought you were going to tear up the seats,' Sandy Daley later said to me.

That was the night I smuggled the Exploding Galaxy into the hotel, helped by Richard (a clerk who still works indispensably at the Chelsea). Roy watched them, silent and attentive. He had never seen or heard anything like them before.

I was beginning to understand his background by now, though his descriptions of it varied from time to time. All I knew for sure was that he came from one of the Southern states, that he grew up in the country and was mad about Johnny Cash and wanted to play the guitar just like him.

To this end, he persuaded me to see a documentary on Cash, sitting close and pointing out the wonders − to him − of the music and singing. Sadly, he could not even tune his own guitar and I had to do it for him. But he sang rather well, his repertoire consisting of songs of sentimental endings, death and unrequited love. Running into well-known musicians like Johnny Winter or Country Joe, he would tell me excitedly of the encounter, like a child. But he was old in the ways of the world. I tried to fill in the gaps in his life, seeing him in a Southern bar, with rednecks, singing Johnny Cash-type songs, laughing and getting drunk. But even that did not fit exactly. He was a wonderful storyteller. The stories were all built around his own escapades and perhaps a few of them were true. But how they made me laugh. He was a marvellous companion.

As time went on, I suggested he might like to look for a job. Loyally he tried. Macy's took him on in the boys' department, but this lasted less than a week. Roy was adept at stealing. It was a sleight of hand which he must have practised all his life. I never knew what small trophy would turn up on my dressing table, deftly lifted from a counter in Woolworth's or a stationer's shop. But his stealing was not entirely accurate. At the end of the week he came home from Macy's with a pair of jeans. The theft might have made some sense had the jeans fitted him; but they were a boy's size and quite useless for his six-foot frame.

After Macy's Roy tried a florist in the garment district. This lasted somewhat longer, and he brought me bouquets of false flowers and many black and white pebbles which I turned over to George for his fish tanks.

[111]

Claiming he could drive a truck, Roy found a job doing just that. But it was one of those immense trailer trucks used for moving entire households of furniture. Roy managed to find the house, but was unable to park the truck. He rang me from time to time during this ordeal, saying he was 'almost there' but in the end gave up and left the truck where it was.

After that there were no more jobs. He stayed bent over his guitar, strumming and singing. He told me he was making an album. He told George he was making an album. He announced the same thing proudly to Sandy. I did not see how he could possibly make an album without money but because he was so mesmerizing in his belief in himself, imagined he had met someone willing to lend a studio and the essential equipment. This was entirely possible, as Roy used to explore the Village when I was away at work. He could very well have met someone.

The day came when he appeared with a record, asking George if he might play it on George's stereo. He was intensely excited. So were we. He could succeed, George said. Yes, yes, I agreed, and both of us ignored the spasms of doubt that might have destroyed the occasion.

We assembled in George's studio. Sandy too was there, Grace Slick of Jefferson Airplane, and several of the band. George told Roy to go ahead. None of us had looked closely at the record. The song began. A good rock sound, an attractive voice. But it was not Roy's. Or was it? At least, no one present recognized the song as anyone else's.

When it finished, we all, including Grace Slick, congratulated Roy, who returned the record to its sleeve. It seems to me now that all of us knew very well he had gone out and bought – or stolen – the song, but some profound, inexplicable loyalty to him, to ourselves, to artists, made it mandatory that none of us would speak of our suspicions. The record disappeared but Roy had had his moment at the Chelsea.

In the early 'Seventies things at MGM were going badly and the day came when I had to pack up my books and typewriter and leave a job I had held for fourteen years, both in London and New York. It was either that, or move with the Story Department to Hollywood. This I would not do. Roy was thoughtful, commiserating and *there*. He helped me to pack heavier things, then diplomatically left the MGM building while I stayed on for a farewell party with some of the more fortunate staff and those who were moving to Hollywood.

My being without work seemed at first to make no difference to our closeness. Roy would accompany me to the unemployment office, and when I was done there he would be waiting at the door, wearing a flak jacket he had no doubt stolen from somewhere to make him look like a Vietnam veteran, of which there were several in every one of the long queues. Many had made incomplete recoveries from their terrible experiences. One day a car backfired and a veteran standing near Roy dropped to the floor, and when Roy helped him to his feet, said in a dazed way that it must have been enemy fire.

I went job-hunting, without success. Roy began mysterious excursions of his own. He brought me money sometimes, insisting he had earned it. Then he began to stay away at night. When he came back to say he had met someone who wanted him to drive her car to the South, I decided ruefully that my time was up. But it was painful the night he disappeared, and I forgot I was middle-aged and expecting too much.

There continued to be no jobs. Mayor Koch was said to be helpful to the unemployed, so I went to see him, on the way telling Stanley, who had become restive as my money dwindled. Koch's secretary denied the possibility of help. I went back to the unemployment queue where I was beginning to make friends. Propinquity and a shared unease resulted in conversation. I heard several stories. One came from a small neatly dressed Chinese-American who told me things had not been so bad since the 'Thirties. He had come to the United States fifty years ago and, as a mechanic, had been earning latterly $4.50 an hour. Now he was offered $2.50 and would probably have to accept it in the end. If Roosevelt were alive today, it would be different, he said.

The black cop in charge liked to chat and he too told me the situation was worse than he had ever seen it. I went on hunting for work and drew my sixty-five dollars weekly unemployment money until time ran out and I looked destitution in the face.

During this time Roy came and went over a period of eighteen months. Belatedly, I began to suspect that he was probably inclined to be a junkie. Yet I never actually saw him take drugs, and there were no marks on his arms. During his absences, telephone calls, charges reversed, began to come in from all over the United States. My telephone bill was huge, and Stanley refused to let me make any more calls from my room. I tried circumventing this by making a note of every call I made daily. They never seemed to tally with Stanley's figures. And still Roy's calls came, professing undying love – like the letter he had left saying that if he had had the money he would have asked me to marry him.

One day he returned, wearing a 'fright' wig of unreal texture and colour. He told Sandy and me that the wig hid the fact that his hair was too short by Chelsea standards. He still desperately wanted to be the great rock star, but his guitar was missing. I let him stay and believed him when he said he had been in prison. He also said he had a brain tumour, which I could not believe. Then began his Mafia period. When he was away for a whole night, he would return to tell me he had been to a Mafia meeting. I asked him to describe it, and vividly saw the enormous hypothetical marble-topped table around which the Mafia sat, preparing to distribute hard drugs wherever they could. Roy seemed quite unaware of the illegality of even his fantasy; he was preoccupied with the power the Mafia wielded. He was proud to be with them.

Of course, in the end it was impossible to believe that he was. It was like the rock record. Yet early one morning he came into the room with a shopping bag filled with many glacine packets of white powder, dumped them on the bed, then went to sleep, saying that he must get up again shortly before going out to 'make his drop'. I was appalled, watching him sleeping, a gaunt, beautiful young man who possessed the imagination of someone halfway between madness and poetry.

Again he disappeared, and this time I was relieved to see him go. The calls began again. He grew abusive when a — to him — strange man answered my phone. He accused me of being unfaithful. I began to dread the calls, and to dread his possible return. It happened. He appeared looking used-up and shabby, and was wearing chunky black and white shoes which he insisted he had been given by an undertaker in whose hearse he had ridden. Again absence, and then the return with a very young wife and baby, both of whom he had acquired in his on-again, off-again visits. By now I was resigned to putting up with this strange relationship which had begun with love. I helped them to buy a bus ticket and sighed with relief, hoping they would never knock again on my door.

But Roy did. He was alone, calm, prosperous-appearing and had a brand new electric guitar which he carried in a grey fur sling, reminiscent of the days of Johnny Winter. He stayed a few days, gave me a small sum of money, then vanished, still vowing eternal love.

By now things had become difficult. I was quite without funds.

[114]

Social Security sent a woman to find out if I was eligible for help. She was young and pleasant and seemed very excited to be within the sacred precincts of the Chelsea. Like the judge during my income tax trial, she confessed she had creative urges. She had always wanted to be a tap-dancer, she said, and executed a few steps on the beautiful old floorboards of my room which had been revealed when the rug had been removed. (I had lent Ed Callahan my room when I was still employed and away in England. He had promised not to bring any of his six cats there, but he cheated and brought a kitten which achieved Tom-hood on the visit and sprayed everything with the signs of his fertility. It was ghastly and nauseating. My friendship with Ed almost ended there and then. But I forgave him when I saw the floorboards.)

Charles James wrote me one of his frequent letters. This time it was typed and very long.

> Dearest Florence,
>   I do apologize for not being able to leave work to come to talk over the disaster befallen you, but the work I had to continue, against a deadline, also related to the same impending disaster which might befall, less than myself, the projects which I have spent ten years getting under way with set-back after set-back . . . in fact each time I felt I was going to be in the clear.
>   I don't know if any of us will weather the storm. Of course I understand the predicament which Stanley has to face, and I cannot blame him, as long as I am indebted to him . . . My own situation is of that sort of 'fragile solidity' that I tend to spend overmuch time worrying about problems I can do nothing about . . .
>   For the first time in decades I was invited to spend a month in Cap Ferrat — all expenses paid, by my earlier sales manager and director, who became a widower on the death of Miss Tilly Marks, a third owner of Marks and Spencer. I felt my commitments here did not permit this respite for even if a long period of rest after so many years were, in any way, beneficial, I would be worrying all the time about the work I had left behind and those who counted on it . . .
>   My telling you my situation does not make yours any better. I know this quite well. You have, however, more friends than I do now, never hardly leaving my room, which has closed in on

[115]

me. During the heat wave I virtually lived in the dark between a crippled air-conditioner and a fan, the sweat drying on me as soon as it poured forth to inundate me. My great soporific was to re-read over and over again the records of a Lady in Waiting during the last years of Queen Victoria; feeling, by doing so, that disasters do not belong to any one period.

Four years ago we all seemed so happy. Now all faces are tinged with the gloom of despair. Twenty-Third Street has less dignity than One-Hundred-and-Twenty-Fifth.

My writing and planning is constantly being interrupted by visits, usually unexpected. I don't know how I function; nor have I ever understood how you after years of security could continue with such abounding, if exteriorized, enthusiasm. That you have done so is an almost startling example of optimism in the face of one defeat after another.

I cannot tell you how much I admire you for keeping up appearances. As so often with me, but not with most people, my affection for you deepened with empathy.

None of these words really will help you. If we were in past days when much money passed through my hands, I would certainly have found a way to pass some of it on to you. Your record of work done with the greatest conscientiousness and solid dedication and talent make it a matter of irony that the big firm for which you worked for many years did not make preparations for your future.

He then offered to write to anyone who might be useful to me —

someone you do not want to contact personally but would like another to do this for you. You have only to ask me. 'Refusal', so often my lot, would mean nothing to me, though I am sure it would destroy your morale for days.

And he continued:

Visit me if you are depressed, there is always time between appointments for a visit which would give me pleasure even if the reason for it were sad; and sometimes two together can think up projects which, alone and depressed, would never occur to them.

[116]

Just call me, and if I am at work in the workshop with a new student you would encourage me to put forth vigour which is becoming foreign to me, and in this you would subconsciously share, and I hope find surcease from your present worries so that you would think, with my prompting of other uses for your talent and wit which you may NOT have thought of under strain.

> With love
> a friend from afar, but nevertheless
> an admirer and friend,
> Charles

He was indeed a friend, helping me draft letters to various organizations that might give me a grant. The letters kept coming and in each he offered hope and courage and affection. But no grant appeared.

Perhaps it was my fault. Perhaps I had gone too far down the dark tunnel in which self-pity makes us lose ourselves. My friends understood and left me alone in the sense that they did not commiserate in a facile way. So many of them had been through the same thing.

There were times, in fact, when the Chelsea tenants, carried on a stream, a flood of misfortune, fell drunken, hit their heads, vomited, knelt desperately, unheeding in their misery. Then, fastidious in despair, they cleaned and polished and searched the corners of their rooms for new hope.

1971 was a strange year. Stanley was stern, but he did not evict me. After being refused telephone service, Irene, my friend and maid, was told not to clean my room or make my bed any more. This restriction led to interesting visits to the cellar and the laundry room to fetch my own clean sheets and to chat with the assembled maids. Their friendliness and understanding helped creeping depression.

For depression it was. Anyone who has gone job-hunting day after day without success knows the eroding result. The Chelsea became a real refuge, even though Stanley grumbled. But among most of my friends, money was short. We went in for high finance. George lent me $5.00, I lent Sandy $2.00 and could not pay back Mark who later asked for his $2.00. Then Gregory persuaded me to lend him $3.00, making it impossible for me to buy Mark a drink. It went on and on. We gave each other food, and Manolo frequently let me have drinks for free. He

[117]

shook his head sadly, portraying an 'Oh, Florence, Florence' feeling. Then he lent me $10.00 without my asking.

But one does survive. Maurice Girodias, the publisher who was living then at the Chelsea, came to my room one day. Maurice was well known for the Olympia Press which began life in Paris under his father, and which was responsible for introducing Henry Miller, Genet, Burroughs, Nabokov and others to the world. He was responsible for *The Story of O* as well. I liked Maurice with his sour Gallic wit. Now he suggested I write a pornographic book for him. The idea appalled me. I dislike pornography. Striving to repeat dirty jokes, I never fail to miss the point. 'Feelthy' books and pictures evoke the sniffy disapproval of my Puritan ancestors. Yet I know it has its place in the course of the world and some of it makes me laugh. I told Maurice I would think about it. As a result of this he left two or three assorted works of erotica in my mailbox with a note saying that these, in his opinion, were among the best and might give me an idea of how to start a novel of my own.

Having just that morning received a dressing-down from Stanley in his cluttered office under the cherubs, I took a tuck in my flaccid courage and sat down to read. To my astonishment I enjoyed them, particularly one by a Swedish writer in which a wandering teenaged boy comes to stay with a happy, but well-behaved, middle-class family. His influence on them in turn results not only in each of them sleeping with him, but in the entire family – not excluding the dogs – ending up in bed together.

I sat down and wrote an outline. Decidedly, it was not the easiest thing I've ever done. Looking back, I think that D.H. Lawrence, whose writing was pure by contrast, did influence me somewhat. But I went way beyond flowers in the navel or elsewhere. The result pleased Maurice and he gave me a contract. Its terms were scarcely outstanding: $1700 and no royalties. But he also gave me an advance. I told a relieved Stanley, and got out my old Olympia.

I had not used it since departing the MGM glass tower and it was in need of new ribbon. This meant a trip to my supplier, something which always amused me. The typewriter shop was halfway between Fifth and Sixth Avenues on Twenty-Third Street. Its general appearance was of disuse, and on one side of the entrance door a display window showed nothing but a Chinese typewriter and a stuffed two-headed calf. This surreal pair never failed to interest me. Once inside, light seemed to vanish. One almost felt one's way to the back of the long dark shop where every kind of office equipment was piled on dim shelves. Presiding over this was a voluminous woman in what I thought of as black bombazine. Despite the confusion and the gloom, she always knew exactly where everything was, right down to type-writer ribbons.

Once I asked her why she kept the monstrous calf. She gazed at me almost with pity, then said, 'Because it's an antique!'

To say that return to writing raised my spirits would be wholly untrue. They not only continued to fall, but managed to fracture whatever control I had over my tear ducts. Waiting for a bus on Twenty-Third Street, I would suddenly start sobbing in a scandalous way, drawing stares, though no comments. New Yorkers seldom comment. Riding on the shuttle where over the years I had grown used to the number of passengers who looked like escapees from numerous Picasso paintings, their features brilliantly deformed so as to make some kind of mad sense, with what seemed to be a Cyclops eye in the forehead, and upside down mouth, a nose set too far to the side, I now found myself wondering how I looked to them.

Something had to be done.

On occasions, I had been to Bellevue to see mentally disturbed or alcoholic friends, once even going by mistake into the morgue which was only a few doors down from the main entrance and easily mistaken. But it was St Vincent's which appealed to me. It was close; they had already saved my life; Chelsea people usually went to St Vincent's in moments of crisis, unless they needed long periods of treatment in Bellevue or Payne–Whitney.

In between turning out salacious chapters of what I had entitled 'Wait for Me I'm Coming', I took myself down to Fourteenth Street and tried to attract attention in the psychiatric wing of St Vincent's. No one could help. There was a waiting list. They took my name and I sobbed my way back home. A severe depression is like a cloud over the mind. I worked; I ate and drank and talked with my friends, but was only partly aware.

Like a leitmotif, calls from Roy would arrive, then Roy himself looking gaunt, but filled with loving remorse. One such arrival was fortuitous. I had assembled a number of sleeping pills and swallowed them all. Roy found me and he and Charles Beard brought me round. No doctor was called. We were, all three, reticent. Roy stayed a few

[119]

days, then took off for who knows where. I went on writing and making daily calls to St Vincent's.

One morning I saw a doctor I'd never seen before. His name was Sandro Olgiati. He was Italian, young and extremely handsome. He was also the first doctor down there who had appeared truly interested in my tear-sodden condition. He listened to some of my woes, though I was not, with the veil over my thoughts, altogether certain of what I said. Then he asked me if I had a friend at the Chelsea who would bring me my clothes. I was shocked. What did he mean? He replied quietly that of course I must come into hospital at once. I rebelled. He was firm. Here, offered to me with sympathy and professionalism, was what I had been yearning for, but my instinct was to run. I stayed. And presently Sandy appeared with a suitcase of my clothes. George was with her. Other friends following. My dear, far-removed-from-the-Chelsea cousins came from uptown. It was a gathering.

Floating on tranquillizers, I felt like the hostess at a most unusual party. But behind the couch and chairs where we sat in what I soon learned to call the 'recreation room' was a catatonic patient named Ellen. She sat, beautiful as an ice maiden, frozen in time, unmoving, unspeaking. Her distance disturbed us all: she was in some far country, like the queen in George MacDonald's *Back of the North Wind*. Then we forgot her and talked and chatted and suddenly my visitors were gone and I was alone, as we all were alone in that new home, the psychiatric ward of St Vincent's Hospital.

By the third week I was drifting with the rest, occupying temporarily an insulated world in which yoga on the roof and the making and baking of ceramic objects in a workroom way down in the bowels of the building were soothingly acceptable activities. I shared a room with a Puerto Rican drug addict who remarked acidly, 'Honey, it's all shit, this methadone. Won't cure anyone. They'll just sell it on the street.'

My fellow inmates were varied. I got to know a few quite well and saw little difference between them and a junkie named Eliot running naked through the Chelsea corridors with flowers in his hair. Some, however, were more dignified. Maria, small and round, nightly knelt in prayer before the television set, annoying some of the others who wished to watch their progammes. The ice maiden melted enough one day to smile, and it was good to see. A well-dressed man of small stature and wild eye whom I thought of as 'Fred' spent long moments trying to telephone his stockbroker from a telephone that had been made deliberately inoperable. Fred did not seem to know, but talked on and on.

He must have found out, however, because one evening he took his revenge. He did not appear at supper but his absence seemed not to be important to the staff until we finished our meal and attempted to open the door to the recreation room for after-dinner coffee. The door was locked. Through the glass panes we saw Fred standing by the piano with a billiard cue in one hand. As we watched, he lifted up the huge coffee urn and poured out its contents on a pile he had made of books, magazines, chess sets, Monopoly and all the games and puzzles awaiting us. Then with his cue he stirred the mess as though preparing a stew in a cauldron. He was still stirring when the charge nurses seized him and hustled him away. He was locked in for the night where recalcitrant patients were sent. It must have been a room on the same floor, for later we heard him singing.

When I left St Vincent's it never occurred to me that I would ever see any of my fellow patients again. But I did — several of them, and one was Fred. It was in the Fourteenth Street subway, when I was waiting for a train. There, down the platform, was Fred busily doing something with a slot machine. Making another call to Wall Street? He appeared to be irritated and shook the machine with both hands. Then he saw me and stopped, darting behind a pillar from which he peered at me with demented eyes. I felt suddenly sad, wondering where and how he had reached his terrible state of anxiety.

Before all this, however, I was brought to my own form of punishment, though I was not locked up. One of the doctors who had originally questioned me after admission, came to me as I was contemplating the pretty coloured titles with which I intended making something — a vase, a dish for pins, something equally important.

'No more ceramic ashtrays for you,' he announced. 'I want you to finish that book because I want to read it.'

I felt very downcast. Ceramic ashtrays were fun — and I had hoped in a vague way never to work on that book again. Had I really told the doctor about it? It seemed I had. He told me I was to return to the Chelsea with a nurse, who would not wear her uniform to save me any embarrassment. Then I was to pick up my typewriter and the unfinished manuscript and return to St Vincent's.

All went as planned. I did see one or two friends in the lobby and said 'hello' to the nurse's surprise. In my room she asked me why I'd done it since the doctor had emphasized camouflage and a minimum possibility of embarrassment. I couldn't tell her that no one at the Chelsea would have cared, that my incarceration would not matter to most of them. They knew it was a case of 'There but for the grace of God . . .'

Back at the hospital I began to work. St Vincent's is a Catholic hospital with the Virgin Mary gazing down benevolently from most of the walls. Under her kindly smile, I set about writing of cocks and cunts while from time to time the doctor came to look over my shoulder. It was indeed writing for my survival, but when I left St Vincent's after six weeks the manuscript was in my suitcase.

Maurice approved, paid me, I paid Stanley what I owed him and began work on another book. There was a subtle change in the Chelsea atmosphere: Black Panthers were being replaced by Black Power. Black Americans took off for Africa where they searched for their roots, returning with African names and souvenirs, not all of which were native to the land of their forbears. The rock star Wilson Pickett was depicted in a documentary about himself, as a new African. An old friend from London, Jan Carew, novelist and poet, born in what was once British Guiana, changed from being a leader of the Black Panthers in Canada to teaching at Princeton. Another West Indian friend, playwright and actor Errol John, turned up at the Chelsea and came to renew acquaintance. I had known Errol when I worked for the MGM London office, when he had written a play *Moon on a Rainbow Shawl* which won the *Observer* drama prize. I had presented the script as a possible movie, but MGM had rejected the idea until Errol won the prize. Then came the cable from Hollywood: 'Get Errol John!' By that time Errol had taken off for Trinidad and subsequent negotiations with his agent fell through. And here he was, handsome as ever.

My dear friend Alice Childress, black playwright, novelist and actress, invited me to her daughter's wedding reception, which was held in a night club in Harlem somewhere. It was joyous. When the Negro Ensemble Company, to which Alice belonged, had a farewell party in a downtown theatre before departing on tour in Europe, I was invited. Coming away inspired, I thought as I had so often thought, of the idiocy of racism which sets out to make it impossible to accept beauty, humour, talent – and love. I felt myself not to be a racist. A few days later, walking up Seventh Avenue just behind a beautiful black girl, I came face to face with three young black men. They were glistening with strength and health and self-importance, as is the way of young men. They momentarily blocked the way, eyes on the girl.

'You're beautiful,' said one, then turned to me, 'but *you're* ugly!'

The desperation I felt after this remark arose from the fact that never, never could I explain to the young man that I understood his loathing just as I understood the burden of my collective guilt. But I could never sit down with him and talk of arcane nonsense that precludes friendship, because he would never believe that I was not part of that nonsense. And, of course, I was.

Not long after this encounter, a black girl threw me down in the subway station at Thirty-Eighth Street and threatened to push me on to the tracks. I think she would have done it if two men hadn't come to my rescue. The fault was again mine. Dreaming, I rode past my own stop and at Thirty-Eighth Street was met by the torrent of workers going home for the day. They kept shoving me back into the car and, when I had fought my way out, this girl, one of the last to give way, turned to find the doors closing. She had missed her train, and this, at the end of a long work day with a long wait for the next train going to Harlem, is cause indeed for anger. But not for the violence to which I was subjected.

The palm of my right hand was gouged and dripping with blood. I stood waiting by the ticket office for a cop, summoned by the black ticket collector. People eyed me. The cop, when he came, was also black, but by the time he arrived my assailant had caught the next train. I felt relieved, but when I was being stitched up – again at St Vincent's – my relief did not prevent anger. How dared she tamper with my life! The young white doctor who was sewing me up said he hoped the incident would not influence my feelings about black people, most of whom were wonderful. I felt the same despair that had pinched me when insulted by the young men in the street. How to explain? My anger at the girl was not because she was a black girl intent on revenge, but because she used unjustifiable violence on my person. She could have been any colour; my anger would have been the same.

I gave up and turned to happier things. Because of many stitches, typing was out for the time being, so I began living again. Spring was giving way to summer. Youth was in the streets. We still heard 'Summer in the City' sung by the Loving Spoonful. Umbrella hats were popular, sold at street corners; so were mirror sunglasses. On a spring Sunday several of us went to Sheep Meadow. There was still a feeling of the recent past when we had all sat together for the great love-in there. Young people everywhere were playing; throwing frisbees, flying superb kites. Colour was overwhelming. Lilac bloomed near the boundary of buildings, unreal behind the delicate green of new leaves. We climbed the glacial smoothness of the huge elephant-grey rocks and sat watching and listening to happy guitar players whose enthusiasm could match Johnny Berger's, if not their ability. He was busking again in the tunnel near the zoo.

Creativity was in the air all over the city that summer. It was always in the air at the Chelsea, winter or summer. People who had no special talent seemed to burst into a kind of revelation of themselves, driven to make, to carve, to paint, to build, everything from metal bookmarks in unusual shapes to plastic bags of strange outline and hue. And there was poetry. Knowledge surfaced, the knowledge that everyone had talent somewhere if he but knew how to use it.

New York at that time was swarming with South Americans, some legal, some not. We got to know one of these, a young, attractive man who delivered fried chicken, potatoes and salad in white cardboard boxes from a restaurant called 'Chicken Delight'. He too became known as Chicken Delight. I used the service and soon discovered that he had romantic notions about me. I found this embarrassing. I also felt that he was better than his job. Dignity had been removed. A Spanish-speaking friend found out that his name was Tony, that he had studied law in Chile, and that, to say the least, he was confused. So was I, when he lay in wait for me in the corridors asking for a kiss. A fractured kind of conversation – his English was not good – brought to light a need in him to write. I suggested a poem. The following was eventually pushed underneath my door.

Poem from Tony

You asked me for a poem
And I am thinking how
To do it as beautifully
As if I were looking at you.

When I think of others
It costs me many verses
But when I think of you . . .
Who doesn't feel inspired!

[124]

Making verses has not been easy
But it costs me nothing
I find enough looking in your eyes
And I feel like a poet.

The sun may go away
And leave sorrow on my youth
But you look at me
And there are no more cloudy days.

I promised you this poem
And I have tried to realize it
In case I do succeed
You must interpret it.

I did. I did. But the discrepancies were such that I failed him. It was one of those times when, adventurer, I let myself and Tony down, and romance.

For a long time, Irene, my erstwhile maid, had been asking me to have dinner with her in her home in Harlem. She said I could bring anyone I'd like, and she would cook us a real Southern-type meal. I invited Sandy Daley, who was for the moment without a lover and also even poorer than I, not having had the dubious advantage of writing a pornographic novel.

We set out on a Saturday morning, Sandy groaning and cursing and now wishing she had never agreed to come. We got off the bus somewhere on Lennox Avenue and walked along the street feeling conspicuous and uncomfortable. Sandy in particular was highly visible, as, lately she had taken to wearing long black or red dresses designed by Halston. Knowing Sandy, she had probably found someone to buy them for her – unless Halston himself gave them to her. These dresses were nothing if not seductive, fitting every curve and hillock of Sandy's fairly substantial figure. Her appearance over the years had altered from slim pre-Raphaelite Dante Gabriel Rosetti (except for the straightness of her long hair, she looked very like La Ghirlandata) to a moderate Renoir. Now our progress was painful. Silence followed us. The Harlem folk of that area were all out on their stoops, sitting in neighbourly Saturday groups, but conversation ceased as we approached. One sensed hostility.

Then someone, a man, asked, 'You girls want a taxi?'

We mumbled something, or I did, and hurried on. There was a suggestion of *double entendre* in the question, and we did not want to know about it.

Irene lived in what had once been one of the truly elegant houses of Harlem, property of well-to-do whites. It had been chopped about, halves of big rooms cut up again so that doors and walls were in the wrong places. Irene's living room was also the bedroom, and the kitchen, a tiny place, gave directly on to this area. By contrast, the bathroom down the hall was large and also spotless. Everything was immaculate.

Irene welcomed us warmly and offered us each a glass of Manische-witz wine. I had tasted it at bar mitzvah ceremonies and found it sweet and heavy. We drank. Irene's husband arrived. He was half Irene's size, a lively sparrow of a man in green trousers and a jacket decorated with green sequins. A son also appeared just as the meal began to arrive on the table. He was in his twenties and Irene seemed very proud of him.

The food kept coming. Spare ribs, fried chicken, corn bread, greens, hominy grits, sweet potatoes, gravy, two kinds of pie. Finally Sandy groaned, said she could manage no more, and went to recline on the bed. Irene's husband found this delightful. He was a vaudeville kind of man and told jokes with great expertise. When we left, there were hugs all around, and the son escorted us to a bus stop.

We had eaten too much for conversation, but when we reached One-Hundred-and-Second Street, Sandy got off, saying she wanted to drop in on some friends. I watched out of the window as we drove off, hoping she would be all right. A flock of black women in white Muslim robes walked towards Sandy in strange juxtaposition. They must have belonged to Muhammad Ali's forces with their new religion of hatred for 'whitey', 'the man', 'honkey'. I felt sorrowful thinking of the happy luncheon we had just finished.

When Sandy saw me that evening, she said she had been unmolested until a swarm of small, black boys surrounded her, chanting and jeering. She had simply laid about them with her shoulder bag and escaped.

Summer advanced and with the heat my writing stumbled. Maurice had vetoed the outline I gave him, saying it was 'not dirty enough'. I laid it aside, substituting love for work. My new friend was a motorcycle freak and computer programmer named John Danishevski. Riding a motorcycle through Manhattan traffic had its disadvantages, proven when he fell off and broke his leg. Hobbling about the apartment in a cast, he seemed quite happy and played with Mexican jumping beans from Japan. With a nasty kind of frugality, the Japanese had cut the beans in half, thus augmenting the amount in the bags in which they were sold. With the insane prodigality of programming knowledge, John knew all about jumping beans, and told me of the little worms inside the beans whose movement caused them to twitch when held in the warmth of a human hand.

'Jumping beans,' he quoted. 'Seed of any Mexican euphorbiaceous plant or the genera *Sebastiania* and *Sapium*, which is inhabited by the larva of a small moth whose movements cause the seed to move about or jump.'

One day, a bean hatched out while John was playing with it. The moth moved as jerkily as it had in the bean, then disappeared. We fantasized, pretending that, hidden in some corner of the room, it would grow to vast proportions and take its revenge one dark night, its huge misshapen shadow appearing on the ceiling.

Broken legs heal, and one day I came home to find a heap of silt and unrolled bandage in the tub. John had not waited for the hospital to remove his cast. From then on, I knew I would lose him. He took his bike and set off for Watkins Glen and the races. He would be camping, he said, but not for long as he must be back on his job.

I missed him, but there were others, and from time to time he reappeared. Even after he got married. The Chelsea and my friends there became of the utmost importance to me at this point. The hotel was a home more than it had ever been. Everyone seemed to feel that way. Worried and flat broke, we gave little parties, the mood flaring up quickly from a conversation or a meeting in the hall. People came to my room to drink and we waxed Russian and threw the glasses out of the window to land on the synagogue roof next door and just below my floor.

A new movie-maker arrived – Les Blank from California. He lived on Poinsettia Street in Hollywood and called his company Flower Films. I thought him very pleasant. He asked if he could show his latest film one evening in my room. Perhaps a few other movie-makers would like to watch. It was a documentary on the black musician Lightning Hopkins. I invited Shirley and Harry Smith and a few others. The evening was disastrous. For the first time I saw the opinions of underground film-makers set against commercialism, although in truth I found 'Lightning Hopkins' charming. When it was over and the lights turned on, Les waited for approbation. Instead Shirley and Harry tossed the reel back and forth like a ball, while its owner watched in horror. Their contempt was evident and painful: the elite speaking.

Another man sailed, like an oil tanker, into my life. He worked for a toy manufacturer and was in line, he told me, to become an executive if he could lose fifty pounds. I felt this to be a good idea because when he took me out to dinner, his awesome width made passage between tables hazardous. I would follow in his wake, seeing cutlery and plates swept to the floor as he churned on, having eaten a meal that sent his hopes of being an executive even further away. But he was kind.

The aura of the Incredible String Band still hung about me; I basked in reflected glory. Teenaged girls came to call and ask questions about my son. One even went to Scotland to find him. More indirect was the call from the head of an air freight company who said he was the father of the group Santana's drummer and would like to take me out to dinner. We must have something in common because of our sons. I accepted and was given a vast sheaf of gladioli that had just been shipped in from somewhere by air freight. They made me feel embalmed.

There were other men, some serious lovers. But Valentine was both exceptional and non-serious. He was a photographer in his twenties, of Russian extraction, a golden boy, funny and wild. With Valentine around, my life was in considerable peril, for he was extraordinarily accident-prone. But he had a gift for making one happy with the absurd and the beautiful combined. He had a habit of appearing suddenly outside my door to announce himself in arbitrary ways, the most unusual of which was with his bicycle. He would ring the bell loudly and wake me up. He photographed me constantly but only gave me one print. It was his bread and butter, he said. This artistic parsimony I had also noticed in the English painter Bernard Hailstone, who asked to paint my portrait but would not let me have it, even for the sum I could then pay him.

One morning Valentine suggested we go to Coney Island together. It was early spring, and cold. The beach would be deserted. I liked the idea and we took the subway like two excited children. Coney Island was revealed in its real beauty. Long white beaches; trees hiding last

[128]

season's swings; and monstrous contraptions for the pleasure of the young. A little red train was still running, and as we watched, it chugged out into the open from a background of trees with the tenderest of green leaves. The train was loaded with small black boys who cheered and waved. At intervals along the beach stood lifeguards' towers. We climbed into one and sat watching the sea until we got hungry. Valentine said he remembered a place where they sold Puerto Rican food. Would I like some pigs' ears?

The pigs' ears were disgusting. Not even worth the effort of a silk purse. But the cook was a charming man. He told us the *Queen Elizabeth II* would be passing soon. Good, Valentine said, we had been waiting for her. The cook looked doubtful. Well, the liner did come quite close to shore, but ... Then he laughed and admitted he had let his imagination run wild. We returned to a lifeguard's seat and imagined the disbelieving expression on the cook's face as we were just in time to see the vast ship float silently past.

I took Valentine with me to a party given by Joyce Elbert, once married to John Hultberg, in her new apartment uptown. For some obscure reason, this party became symbolic, representing for me something final, although at the time I did no more about these feelings than buy a new dress. Yet this itself was symbolic, considering the dress. It was French, blue-checked and with a very tight bodice and puffed sleeves. Too juvenile, too youthful by far. The party was a success, although Valentine drank too much. I felt our uneven but living friendship was coming to an end. Probably because of this, I agreed to meet another man later and to go with him the following morning to see *Le Chagrin et la Pitié*.

On the way home in a taxi, Valentine told the driver to stop. We were on Fifth Avenue beside the park. Valentine jumped out. It was a clear, starry night. He ran into the park with a whoop and began leaping about. A nearby tree attracted him, and he ran round and round it in a drunken state of joy. As I watched, Time lurched with a jolt and a grinding into the season and slot of my old age. I later forgot the moment for a long time, but something had changed.

That was the summer of 1973. Still just in funds from my book, I decided to take a trip to England. By now Valentine, misbehaving, had been asked by Stanley to leave. But he returned several times to see me. On one occasion he brought me a lethal-looking knife, asking me to keep it for him. He felt manic and feared he might hurt himself or

[129]

someone else by accident. I took the knife reluctantly and dropped it into the depths of a big shoulder-bag I carried at the time.

Sandy had planned to come with me, but at the last moment decided against it. At Kennedy Airport, I discovered I had her ticket instead of mine, and the resulting prolonged explanations made me late in boarding the plane. This was the time of bombings and terrorist activities. It was the beginning of luggage being scanned for guns or other weapons. The last aboard, I was stopped anyway and as the official played his instrument over my bag I suddenly remembered Valentine's knife and saw all chances of my trip vanishing to be replaced by arrest and prison. Perhaps because I was late, and the official in a hurry, the knife went undetected. When I reached London, I threw it in the Thames.

NINE

FULL MOON AT THE CHELSEA

THE film *The Godfather* had captured everyone's imagination. I thought of Roy and wondered if he had seen it, sitting in the theatre, identifying himself with his heroes. Down in El Quijote, a kind of Spanish Mafia was gaining power. Every night a man called Casals had a drink, took a corner table, and held forth. He was small, unprepossessing, with brown hair and glasses, and he never seemed to smile. His wife Antonita was the opposite – comely and plump and considerably taller than her husband. She was friendly and told me tales, making me feel quite ill by her detailed descriptions of how to cook bull's testicles – a delicacy, she assured me. Meanwhile, Casals roamed the restaurant, casting a predatory eye about him while Manolo wiped glasses unnecessarily and told jokes in Spanish, laughing too loudly. Something was up.

Then Big Gilbert was taken away to jail for nefarious dealing. Young Gilbert, who had been in the Marines, took his place. Casals looked more important than ever.

In the Chelsea, the atmosphere was mixed. Most of us were still poor and unsuccessful, but John Hultberg emerged from Payne–Whitney and the following year had a retrospective show of paintings at the Martha Jackson Gallery on East Sixty-Ninth Street. He and Lynne were exploring SoHo with a view to buying a loft. But Lynne came often to visit me, to have a meal, to sit and gossip while sewing her jewel-like patchwork cushions for me. Joyce Elbert, whose party had filled me with such a sense of an age having passed, remarked that 'my third husband's fourth wife is sewing Florrie's cushions'.

My own incarceration in St Vincent's had gone apparently unobserved, although Charles wrote me:

Dear, dear, Florence,

I've tried many times in the last 3 (?) days to get in touch with you . . . to know how you are and fear that my having found you

always out means that you may have sought a few days of
refuge from a situation no one but psychiatrists and medication
can resolve. Let me know if you are all right. Although we are
not close friends I appreciate you, am fond of you and
understand your difficult situation . . . I have felt encouraged by
the way you have *stood up* to *circumstances* – shall I say 'gallantly'
even when not for your own good. Let me know how you are.
Affectionately, yours from the sixth floor – Charles

I wasn't sure what he meant about standing up to circumstances
even if it wasn't for my own good, but was inordinately grateful to a
good friend.

Throughout the Chelsea at this time, there was a feeling of mild
panic. Stanley even started taking in pimps again, as well as a
hooker or two. These last were highly theatrical, in particular one
who wore knee-high violet boots, a multi-coloured fur coat that
looked like feathers, bright yellow silk pants and hair intricately
braided.

We all spent a lot of time in El Quijote, spinning out one drink as
long as possible, eating the little sausages that were served hot at the
bar for the early evening crowd. One could make a meal that way. We
listened to the waiters' conversations, or to heated arguments between
strangers. Older men liked to talk of the Depression – reminded
perhaps by the current one – remembering Franklin D. Roosevelt.
'That cripple' said someone, and brought instant retaliation: 'At least
when he stood up he wasn't a cripple.'

There was the Civilian Conservation Corps, wasn't there? Look how
that worked. A younger man was sceptical. 'But you've got to believe,'
cried the Roosevelt supporter.

Over the years, many of us had made good friends through bar
conversations, and now I made a new one. He was a Greek named
Euripedes Laglos and would leave little notes in my mailbox when I
was out.

Florence,
I am, well . . .
Euripedes

He wrote poems too.

[132]

My buzzer does not buzz
My pockets do not jingle
I'm in the Automat
Without my cat —
I borrowed this lined sheet of
Paper from a nervous neighbour
Sporting a sterile briefcase
Obviously, an engineer
Or perhaps a tightrope walker.

Euripedes took me to Greek restaurants where I danced in a circle with elderly men, our arms around each other's waists, to rhythmic Greek music. Then I made another new friend, also acquired in El Quijote: Ron Wertheim was a successful writer and producer of porno films and told me some startling facts about the latter. They did not make me anymore inclined to get on and finish the second novel I had begun for Maurice Girodias. But I did. By today's standards, it was mild. No one bought it and I considered with relief that my days as a porno writer were finished. No Norman Douglas I. But my first attempt had sold out, even with the new title, which Maurice had changed from *Wait for Me I'm Coming* to *The Naked and the Nude*. I stole copies out of the warehouse for friends and family, feeling they were owed to me since I would not receive royalties.

There were compensations for our general poverty that year. The MacDowell Colony held an annual cocktail party for its members, either at the Yale, Harvard or Princeton Clubs. I had always attended them, liking to meet old friends. This year it was to be at the Princeton Club. We were allowed one guest. I invited Sandy to come along. The first round of drinks was always free, then we had to buy our own or, we hoped, have drinks bought for us.

There were little tables in the bar, and we sat waiting for it to open. People began wandering in and, observing them, I thought how the MacDowell image had changed since my last visit there. These folk were so well-dressed, in white trousers and navy blue jackets. The girls wore smart dresses. Strange. We were joined by two young men as we started our first free drink. They insisted on buying the second round, and I mentioned that it was odd that none of my old friends had turned up.

The men with us asked the inevitable question. Where did we think

[133]

we were? It was not the MacDowell Colony party, it was the annual meeting of the New York Yachting Insurance Company. Hence the clothing.

Sandy and I, feeling relaxed, went home in a taxi. On the way we thought how we could work out an entire system of free-drink calls, based on there being innumerable, or at least a good number of, organizations which held parties similar to the one we had mistakenly attended today, and the MacDowell's Colony's, all over Manhattan. We could have free drinks for months, had we so wished.

Soon after finishing my porno book, I came back from a walk to find the lobby littered with cables. It was a camera team from the BBC sent to film an interview with Germaine Greer, whom I knew had moved in to the Chelsea, though I had not yet met her. One of the BBC crew spotted me and hurried over.

'And what do *you* do?' he asked.

This was a question the indoctrinated never ask, and one that the residents, if asked, hated to answer. It was an invasion of hard-earned privacy, a walking of heavy feet over vulnerable turf, like the suffering grass in the seminary gardens.

'I write pornography,' I said coldly.

He seemed delighted. 'Great, great. I'm sure Germaine would like to talk to you,' and started to lead me towards the cameras.

I jerked free, and ran out again into the street, then walking round the block and finally deciding, as vanity overcame scruples, that I would appear on the screen with the famous Germaine Greer. But by the time I got back, the shooting was over. I had lost an opportunity. This was not cause for too much regret until my children wrote from London that they had seen the lobby of the Chelsea Hotel and Germaine Greer. Sadly, I was not there. So much for false pride. I did finally meet Germaine Greer. We had dinner. She tended to lecture.

The Godfather went on playing to an enthusiastic audience. The leading actors turned to other films, but there remained a number of bit players who seemed to feel their finest hour had come and gone without enough recognition. Three of them turned up at my door one morning towards lunch time. I recognized only one of them: the young actor who had played the boy who carried flowers to the hospital. I was at a loss to know what to say to them. And how did they know that once I had worked for MGM? They bubbled with a combination of apology

[134]

and enthusiasm. Perhaps I knew someone who could find them parts in a new picture. I said I was out of touch. They persisted, sitting on the floor at my feet, looking at me beguilingly. I felt desperate and rang Sandy's room. She came down at once, garbed in a red gown. Italian joy prevailed. In turn she sat in the big chair, they at her feet. Now the talk was not about parts in a film, but of food and love and theatre.

They finally left; thanks to Sandy, not wholly disenchanted.

Irving Baer, the hotel's one stockbroker, also left, to live in San Antonio, Texas, with an English woman to whom I had introduced him. This left only one other businessman who had moved in that same year. His name was Willy Schilling and he occupied the room where the man who decapitated dolls had lived. I was happy to have Willy close at hand. Sometimes at night, when fear and nerves were particularly troubling, I would think, 'Good,' hearing footsteps but no knock on my door. 'Willy and I are home for the night.'

Life went on in our mutually uninhibited way. But it limped badly for a time when Charles Beard decided to leave the Chelsea after so many years in order to get married. We wondered each in turn how we would get along without him. There were few of us he had not helped in some way or another: seeing we got enough to eat when ill; making certain we did not miss trains or planes or appointments; walking dogs; baby-sitting; generally casting oil on troubled waters, always with humour and uncondescending wisdom. He was a father figure and we resented his departure although we were paradoxically pleased that he was at last going to lead his own life. He must have rejoiced in his new freedom; possibly he missed us.

The drug scene was diminishing, even if only in the sense that the excitement and even the happiness accompanying a smoke or a snort seemed to have submerged by a kind of dreariness. The girl with the waterbed who had once come to me for valium returned from a cure looking well but soon succumbed again. It was certainly the sole waterbed in the hotel. A Chelsea waterbed supplied by the management would have sprung a leak instantly or be found to contain miniature alligators of the variety allegedly found in the Manhattan sewers. I still wondered sometimes about the Mexican jumping bean that had hatched out and remembered with considerable pleasure the small black mice that Roy and I had discovered in the oven – before the gas was lit. They were definitely town mice with a taste for the sybaritic things in life. We filled the top from a jar with straight whisky and listened to the sounds of frolic and dissipation. Squeak and scrabble, small claws on greasy pan, alcohol going straight to mouse head.

One mouse became very bold and would emerge to dart across the carpet to a far corner of the room while we sat silently and watched. I grew quite fond of the mice. They disappeared when Roy left. Perhaps he took them with him to turn into white horses for his carriage that would transport him to some great mansion where his Mafia brotherhood kept a place for him at the head of their marble-topped table; where Johnny Cash opened his arms to a comparable if not a better guitar player; where old-fashioned emotion was the norm, love written in gold on red velvet Valentines or in blood by the side of a crushed motorcycle ('Tell Laura I love her'); where one stole with impunity because one was so very good at stealing; and where Roy was *le Roi* always and forever.

Sitting in George's room one afternoon, remembering Roy and his famous non-record, I realized that I was as incapable of understanding his drug-induced hallucinations as was George's turtle, its head on a long neck raised above the water, swaying constantly to unheard music.

In the summer of '73, people around us tended to die. It was an extension of Stella's theory that at the full moon everyone went crazy. That summer the moon, though it wasn't, seemed permanently full. Next to the small supermarket, where we did most of our shopping for food, was a little store owned by an elderly white-haired man who sold handbags and belts. He looked like a close relative of the man who ran the supermarket, and who had concentration camp numbers tattooed on one arm. Coming out of the market one morning I saw a large young cop holding the old man tenderly. The windows had been smashed, the shop robbed.

Then, only a few weeks later, picking up coffee and Danish for my breakfast, I saw a yellow police tape had been tied across the old man's door, and on the sidewalk in front of the shop was a dark splash of blood and a chalk mark shaped like a human body. The old man had been shot, I was told, for the sake of six dollars, presumably all he had left from the previous robbery.

The first time I saw a chalk mark it was a shock, a cold divination of general mortality, laid out like a child's drawing, but expressing violence. There had been a chalked outline in the Chelsea corridor

[136]

when the Mafia made its killing too late for the FBI to intervene. We lived cheek by jowl with violence, but as a neighbour it also became a familiar.

There were further compensations within the Chelsea walls. Juliette gave her beautiful parties; Ivan Passer, the Czech film director living at the Chelsea alongside Milos Forman, decided he wanted to read the novel rejected by Maurice Girodias. For a short time I scented fame, imagining a movie. But Ivan politely returned the book and I retired from even a suggestion of limelight into deeper and more comfortable shadow.

In the spring of 1972, Clifford Irving surfaced with his outrageous scheme to write a bogus life of Howard Hughes, choosing to live at the Chelsea Hotel with Richard Suskind, his partner, and his wife, Edith. When found out, he attracted media from all over the country and the lobby was chaotic with the tangled cords and hulks of TV equipment. Suskind went off to jail, and Irving soon followed. There remained Edith Irving and the Irving children. The children were better known to us than their parents, although we knew Edith Irving was a painter. Scheduled herself for prison, she tried gallantly, one could say, to right a few wrongs by holding an auction (at Stanley's suggestion) in the Chelsea lobby. Evidently she had worked all night, for paint on some of the pictures was still wet, the canvas warping.

Arthur C. Clarke made the first offer of $500 while the TV cameras aimed their eyes at his pleasant, civil-service face. Their brilliance matched his own. Stanley, standing on a chair, pleaded with spaniel eyes and worried voice for more bids. But though the lobby was crowded, few pictures sold. It was all wishful thinking. All of it; from conception to misconception. Perhaps the person who engaged one's sympathy more than any was Stanley, who must have come out of the affair considerably poorer, publicity notwithstanding.

After serving seventeen months of his two-and-a-half-year sentence for his part in the fraud, Irving was released on parole and went off with Valdy, an attractive German divorcée who lived with her children at the Chelsea. Edith Irving was also released after fourteen months in a Swiss jail.

By now my peculiar breakup, or breakdown, seemed to have healed. I no longer felt like the song sung by Nilsson: 'Everybody's talking at me/I can't hear a word they're saying/Only the echoes of my mind.'

[137]

Life was good, though penurious. Yet there was still an uneasiness. Perhaps artists are never content, wanting extensions of time, emotion, happiness. I sometimes thought people stoned and in a world of their own achieved a kind of contentment. But, of course, it was induced, and must go on being induced.

Rumours began. The Chelsea was to be sold. That was a permanent rumour. Then came another, far more possible. It gained in momentum, became reality. South of the Chelsea was a parking lot. For those who lived on that side of the building, the view was clear, looking right down to the tip of Manhattan. Now, we heard, the lot had been sold and in its place would be the blinding walls of an apartment building. We were shocked and held indignant meetings. Useless: the rumours were true.

Before long, only thirty feet from the Chelsea's fine old walls, a monstrous yellow machine snuffled and gobbled and spewed out boulders. Manhattan is, after all, built on rock. We watched feverishly. Grey, small ghosts of past dwellers in the buildings surrounding the parking lot were flushed from their holes by a great fart of dynamite, only to be chewed and trampled by the hideous bulldozer. The buildings became rubble, and then there was an interlude of silence as though the destroyers had not yet made up their minds what to do.

Simultaneously, my own past abruptly returned to be, like our peace of mind, torn down and exposed. In a copy of *Time* magazine I came across a full-page advertisement for small ranches gouged out of what had once been my home, the Trinchera Ranch in south-east Colorado. Here, on 255,000 acres of virgin land, fenced and stocked with cattle by my father, I had lived for sixteen years. It had changed hands several times after my father lost it towards the end of the Depression. Now its latest owner was Malcolm Forbes of *Forbes Magazine*, and he was selling bits of it off to land-hungry people.

I knew what the phrase 'sick at heart' meant. There was no possibility of my being reasonable. Emotion prevailed. I had written and published a book about the Trinchera and now sent off one of my few remaining copies to Mr Forbes at his business address, *Forbes Magazine*, not all that far from the Chelsea. It was a belatedly defensive gesture.

My friends were interested. Malcolm Forbes! They knew about him, though I didn't. In reply, I received several letters in turn, one of them from the eldest Forbes son, Christopher, known as Kip, who arrived one day to see me. He was very young, brisk and enthusiastic. We talked about his father's Fabergé collection and his new wife – or wife-to-be – and her Schloss in Germany. She too had seen her past vanish and, he said, he understood how I felt about Trinchera. I wondered if he did, but he was *sympathique*. He said his father wanted a book from me. But the terms were dubious. Two months later, another visit. No book, but they would like any photographs of the ranch I might want to sell.

My next visit from a Forbes was in the person of Bobby, the youngest son. Tall, large, with long blond hair. More discussions. Finally, I sold them some photographs for an archive Malcolm Forbes wished to make. The payment was $1000 which made it possible to settle with Stanley.

Drew Adams, a new friend and an opera buff, took me to a dress rehearsal of *Romeo and Juliet* with Placido Domingo at the Lincoln Center. He wanted to raise my spirits. I felt that in selling the photographs I had betrayed my past, sold out. But what does one do with forty-seven cents until the next social security cheque? I wrote short film scripts for movie-making friends; I typed and was given $200 by an unhinged businessman whose family telephoned accusing me of being some kind of gold-digger. By then, Stanley had the cheque and I was safe for a little longer.

There were memorable parties that summer of '74. Juliette contrived gourmet meals out of very little. 'Cody', a handsome young Texan who habitually wore white linen suits, a white, frilled shirt and white boots, all topped by a white Stetson, often came to my room to talk. He also made parties out of his visits, snorting cocaine from a peacock feather – he refused any other method – and ordering three cases of Heineken at a time. We assumed he had money, being a Texan, but when he disappeared some months later and there was a big robbery at the Plaza, Sandy, for some reason, was certain he had done it. I could not agree, though who knows? With my love affair with Roy that was by turns intense and withdrawn; with the long, hot summer; with most of us existing on faith in ourselves and little loans, some of which were returned, 'Cody' as a thief might be perfectly in tune.

The Incredible String Band gave their last concert at the Bottom Line, a night club. Robin Williamson played the fiddle like the wild Scotsman he is. All of them performed with the kind of perfection arising from knowledge that it was, indeed, the last time they would be together. Shortly afterwards, the band broke up.

Keith Cuerden, Charles James's companion, released from hospital, came to see me. We took a long walk into the Battery. On an abandoned wharf where an old ship was still tied up and where young mothers once – in the late 'Sixties and early 'Seventies – used to play with their small children, hundreds of homosexuals milled about, cruising, talking, strutting, a bizarre mating dance. It was disturbing. There was a concealed violence, and this same kind of violence invaded the Chelsea a few months later. On my way downstairs on a Monday evening in November, I was stopped by the police. My neighbour down the hall, Billy Maynard, who had lived quietly with his close friend, another young man, had been murdered – beaten to death and strangled. Billy had been a photographer, specializing in rock groups and transvestites, like the Cockettes. He was from San Francisco, gentle, kind, always good-natured. I liked him very much.

That same evening, the following notice appeared on the bulletin board with a picture of Billy attached:

$5000 REWARD!
On Monday evening, November 25, 1974
Billy Maynard was killed
In Room 803 at the Chelsea Hotel.
Any person having seen the victim
prior to 10:00 p.m. on Monday, November 25, 1974
or having any information at all
concerning this matter,
please call 753-5343 between 8 a.m. and midnight
or 741-5829 to 8 a.m.
A $5000 reward will be given
for any information
leading to arrest and conviction
of the killer.

It was distressing and unnerving. Something was winding down, but not for long. Creativity burst out again. Harry Smith invited me down for a drink to hear the tapes he was making of Aleister Crowley's poems with Matthew on guitar. Matthew was a long-time Chelsea inhabitant of diffuse talents, not helped by drugs. He was thin and dark, with an engaging smile, always filled with plans which somehow did not materialize. He was a true and dedicated artist; he could have lived no other way than he did. While we were listening to the tapes, Allen Ginsberg came in. When the tapes were finished, we sat around talking, drinking and smoking — at least the men smoked grass. I had given up smoking tobacco and the pleasures of a marijuana high were no longer attainable. It would have been defeating my purpose. Harry, always hospitable, understood.

Around this time, Ed Callahan found himself an apartment not far away to house himself and his cats. We often took walks together, watching the old men playing checkers in the little park off Eighth Avenue. A friend at the Chelsea asked me to keep her company before she went off for a cancer operation. Thank God it was successful. The bulletin board had a laconic notice: 'I'm not programmed for Christ.' In El Quijote, Casals was now blatantly in charge. The Spanish Mafia had arrived. In Sancho Panza they had a Mother's Day party to which I was invited. One young man, handsome and black, looked at me kindly and said: 'You are Life, and one must respect Life.' He meant well.

There were occasions when New York violence, seeping into the Chelsea, inspired loathing even of the hotel. It was the circumstances that caused the violence that upset one the most. My mind, on these occasions, would circle around past elegance when there were champagne days, when Isadora Duncan danced at private parties, and the hotel guest book read like *Who's Who*. Then I went upstairs to one of the penthouse apartments to visit Marguerite Gibbons.

Marguerite had been a dancer, a painter, a singer. Now, after an operation for cancer that cruelly twisted her face, she had retreated, but there was still something life-giving about her. I would come away feeling renewed.

What, after all, was the difference between yesterday's violence and today's? Stanford White and Jim Fisk had been murdered and blood had been freely shed during Prohibition. The great actresses crossing Twenty-Third Street to Proctor's would have pulled their skirts aside to avoid touching sleeping winos in the twentieth century. But in the nineteenth, street sweepers with brooms would have had to run ahead of elegance to brush aside the horse manure. Was not everything equal? Even if it wasn't, the thought that it might be made me feel better. Besides, we had our own champagne days.

[141]

It seemed now as fall grew into winter that an end of something beside the season was approaching. We spent a lot of time in El Quijote, but even there a change had taken place. We listened and drank sangria and wished Manolo did not look so sad. The waiters too had descended into a collective mood of indecision. They would not answer the telephone except under persuasion, even if it might mean a booking.

I got to thinking of the writers I had known at the Chelsea. Alan Sharp, author of 'A Green Tree in Gedde', was one of the first. Others I had not met had written about the hotel. Paul Bowles, a writer/composer, wrote in his book *Without Stopping*, 'Once arrived, we went to the Chelsea Hotel,' where he wrote the score for one of Orson Welles's plays. Bowles must have found what he wanted at the Chelsea, for he returned several times. And there was Patricia Highsmith, the suspense writer. She was quiet, removed, with straight black hair and a lean quality. We often rode in the elevator together, but scarcely exchanged a word. She was a constant worker and subsequent great success seems to have been the result. And there was Charles Jackson, author of 'The Lost Weekend', which became a classic film with Ray Milland in the lead. Perhaps it was Charles's highest point. Nothing he wrote afterwards made such an impact. He was quiet and concerned, once saying to me after a recent suicide, 'Each man has his own perogative but this one took advantage of his privileges.' Not long before he himself died he gave me a copy of his last novel.

Young visitors turned up from time to time, a new generation, forerunners possibly of today's 'yuppies'. They stood about in the lobby, apparently not expecting too much, obviously loving the atmosphere. 'Man,' they would say, 'it's Humphrey Bogart. Wow! It's a movie hotel in Berlin.'

Even Sancho Panza seemed in a bad way. I listened to a man complaining about the mussels he had ordered from the tank in the window. 'The ones we ate were exhausted like they hadn't been carried to the table by the waiter, but like they walked from Long Island, sweating all the way.'

Doris Chase and George Kleinsinger gave a combined party, during which Doris showed her latest teaching films. The turtle danced; Harry Smith and Peggy Biderman, drunk on G and S and stoned on grass, roamed the corridors singing 'Tit Willow' at the tops of their voices. A splendid pimp dressed like an Indian prince asked for change at the desk.

Some evenings in El Quijote it was so quiet that one could hear the rushing sounds of traffic and the persistent buzz of the switchboard next door. We who were poor continued to order our *caldo gallego*, or *gazpacho Andaluz*, or *paella Quijote*, the cheapest things on the menu. No one even considered roast beef any more.

Christmas was imminent. The soiled silver tree appeared again and on Christmas Eve several of us went up as usual to George's to see his film again, *The Little Star*, about the Nativity. It had a moderating effect, acting as a palliative in our often fraught existence, and suggesting innocence and hope. We always came away feeling better and also a little drunk.

On Christmas Day I received a call from Joyce Elbert who had moved from her uptown apartment into the Royalton Hotel, haunt of writers, on Forty-Fourth Street. She was successful now, but far from happy. I found her suffering from a hangover and a suicidal mood. Malcolm Forbes's son, Bobby, had brought me a bottle of Asti Spumante on his last visit, so I took it along and we drank it, moving on to Scotch later. I failed to understand Joyce's despair. She told me, as we sat muzzily talking, that her new contract was for $150,000. Perhaps it was the thought of having to live up to, or write up to, that huge amount of money.

On Boxing Day, Mildred invited me to dinner at Scotty's to be followed by a charming production of *The Rivals*. It was, Mildred said, my Christmas present. On New Year's Eve, Juliette had an eggnog party. She had lit the fire and the room was fragrant with the smell of burning wood. Everyone was joyous and there was no time to remember Charles James's letter to me in which he said: 'Four years ago we all seemed so happy . . .'

By the end of January, 1975, I knew I would have to leave my home of nearly eleven years. The financial struggle continued and there seemed no mitigating possibilities. No grants; no stories sold; outlines of books turned down. All my friends wanted to help, which made me even sadder, knowing how much I would miss them. A great wind from the North tore up the sky and clouds loaded with snow blew over the city. I watched them from my window and thought that Checkpoint Charlie would soon cease to exist.

Mildred Baker gave me a send-off party which was invaded by

[143]

Virgil Thomson, demanding to know why he had not been invited. Presents and sums of money were given me. Juliette paid the bill for my air freight. I was overwhelmed and spent some of the money on a farewell party of my own the very last night. Almost all my albums and books were given away because it was too expensive to take them to England. Bobby Forbes turned up for the party wearing a bright yellow oilcloth jacket and carrying a bottle of champagne. My beautiful cushions from Lynne Drexler had to stay behind, and my record player.

The people I loved arrived and we drank the champagne, sitting on the bed and the floor and the two chairs. A poet named David Hamburger who turned up from somewhere drove me to Kennedy Airport and put me on the plane. Thus I left the Chelsea, my heart and New York City behind me on February 5, 1975. Later, someone wrote me that the last Checkpoint Charlie party went on until after six a.m.

I have been back twice to the Chelsea since then. Once, fleetingly, in 1981, when it seemed as if I had never been away. Mildred gave another party. Then, in the summer of 1984, after contracting to write this book, I flew again to New York and went straight to the Chelsea. Herman, a Puerto Rican clerk whom I knew well, was on duty. It was a Saturday and Stanley, as customary, had stayed at home in New Jersey. Stunned and stupid from jet-lag, I heard someone call my name, and turned to see Matthew.

'Hi, Florrie,' he said. 'You haven't changed.'

Nor had he, nor had he. Then the elevator door opened and out stepped Shirley Clarke. 'Hello, Florrie,' she said. 'Welcome home.'

Herman said he only had a room for $50 a night. Too exhausted to discuss the matter, I took it. Perhaps on Monday when Stanley arrived, some arrangement could be made. It was old times. I wondered if we would again discuss things under the chipped cherubs in his office. My room was on the ninth floor this time, down the corridor from Virgil, but on the same side. The view was superb. Those buildings we had all so dreaded back in 1973 were not so high after all, though they came as far as the sixth floor. But from my window now I could see once more right down over Greenwich Village the full length of the island, and it was beautiful and nostalgic. However, the curtains would not draw, being a skimpy width, each of some cheap orange material. The air-conditioner did not work except to blast out a roaring noise designed to keep sleep far away. There was no tap for the

Marat-Sade bathtub, the lavatory leaked and there was no hot water.

A new, somewhat intoxicated bellman had brought up my big case. He fixed the lavatory but could do nothing about the rest. The maids — in the morning, he said, hopefully for us both. But there was the view, and there were two beds, one double, one single. I mourned that my lifestyle was now so limited. With the window wide, I sat for a time looking out at the wonderful, seductive lights of New York City. I was indeed home again.

Not long before leaving Edinburgh — my home after the Chelsea — I was waiting for a bus. Astonishingly, the lilting of a penny whistle sounded, reminding me of the Incredible String Band. Two young men approached the bus stop, one tall, the other small with red hair and beard. It was he who played the whistle. We talked. When the redhead learned I would soon be leaving for New York and that my destination was the Chelsea Hotel, he immediately asked if I knew Eugénie Gershoy on the tenth floor. He had recently been to visit her.

The incident so well illustrated what Jakov Lind said about the international Bohemian circuit: 'See you at the Chelsea.'

Jonny was delighted by the story when I told it to her in her penthouse studio. Remarkable as ever, she was still working, but had been very ill. I asked her about Marguerite Gibbons and was saddened to hear that Marguerite had given up the fight and flung herself out of the window to become another chalked silhouette.

Charles James had gone too, dead of pneumonia just before a big retrospective showing of his wonderful gowns, some of which are in a permanent collection at the Victoria and Albert Museum. And George Kleinsinger had been taken by cancer.

I spent a long time with his young widow, Susan, a tall golden kind of girl. We talked first in George's studio, the big teak fan whirling above George's Mason and Hamlin grand piano, the source of so much pleasure for all of us. The walls were still peeling; little birds fluttered in their cages; the fish tanks serrated the late afternoon sun shining through the skylight.

There was a staircase now, leading from the studio to the roof which had been made off-bounds to everyone but the penthouse dwellers. It was a new kind of elitism, not popular with those on the floors below. Viva, it seemed, had fought to change the situation but without success. But the gardens flourish, vines and little trees growing in abundance. We took the studio stairs to the roof and sat down on a white garden bench amid the plants and flowers. Susan was certain their richness was due to George. Because of his love for the hotel he had asked that his ashes be scattered in the roof garden and she felt that his spirit, with that special quality of joy he extended to others, now flourished in the blossoms and vegetation he had so greatly loved.

I walked to the parapet to look out at the Hudson River. Sunset was approaching. It would have been easy to succumb to nostalgia and sorrow for the friends with whom I had shared other afternoons and sunsets, but I fought it back. For the moment. It never did to dissemble at the Chelsea; one was soon found out.

Back in the studio, we played George's *Lament and Jig* which he had written for Brendan Behan, and Susan gave me a tape of it to take away. Then we closed the door on the past and went downstairs to have a drink in El Quijote where new and different Spaniards prevailed. Gone Manolo and every one of my old waiter friends. Yet, despite a certain indifference, it seemed to me that given time and familiarity, these Spaniards too might become friends. Or would they? The others, after all, had been exposed to flower power and the lovely craziness of the 'Sixties. Today materialism and piety were rampant.

Another evening, I sat in El Quijote having a drink with Helen Johnson. We talked of old times and of Helen's book on black theatre. She had lived eighteen years in the hotel; I, about eleven. She would never live anywhere else; I had been forced to leave through circumstance. We talked of Eubie Blake, John Bubbles the tap-dancer, and Kid Thompson, now ninety-six years old. Then came another Chelsea anecdote which involved me, though I had forgotten it — if I had ever really known about it.

Helen was one of the generous friends who gave me money to see me on my way. Her contribution was twenty dollars. But I never took it. Somehow, in the chaos of departure, it got left on an El Quijote table, mixed in with the linen. But one of our waiter friends must have seen the transaction and traced the bill. It was returned to Helen who now referred to it as 'laundered money'.

When I made an appointment to see Virgil Thomson, he asked me to bring Mildred. To me he looked just the same. I told him I had just read a book about Sylvia Beach and the 'Lost Generation' in Paris in which he was featured. He snorted. That lost generation was silly, he said. War made lost generations, because the people involved had no jobs to go to. He showed me some paintings he had acquired and talked happily of Scotland. 'I stopped in Glasgow. Every other building was a pub and there were lots of signs with the name Thomson spelled right.' Before I left, he gave me an album of his 'Piano Portraits' and signed it with his name, 'To Florrie, warmly.'

Shirley Clarke and I spent a long hour together, she generously taking time out from working on her documentary about Ornette Coleman, a kind of musical journey, she said, with Coleman's son Bernardo who, at eleven years old in 1968, had been his father's drummer. Shirley sat in her big, wicker Singapore chair telling me enthusiastically about different cinematic forms. We were surrounded by movie equipment in her new room on the eighth floor at the back. Shirley said she had left soon after I did, but loathed Los Angeles and had to come back. The telephone rang. It was her sister, Elaine Dundy in London. Elaine had been married to Kenneth Tynan and it had been the Tynans who first told Shirley about the Chelsea. Elaine had written a best-seller called *The Dud Avocado*, and now was asking Shirley to make a film of it. Shirley said judiciously that she would think about it.

Stanley turned up on Monday, greeted me with surprising enthusiasm considering the trouble I had caused him in the past. I said I would have to leave, being unable to pay so much.

'Florence, I don't want you to leave,' he announced and darted out to the front desk where he told a surprised and pained clerk ('My God!') to halve my bill. Marvellous. I chatted with Eve Tabor, still Stanley's amanuensis, who was finding life with computers more than she could stand. They made mistakes, she said, all the time. Above us, the chipped cherubs played as usual. The office was in its usual clutter. Nothing had changed.

Stanley had been receiving a lot of publicity lately, most of it good. The Chelsea had celebrated its centennial. Here I feel a certain discomfort. In my research I found the hotel was built in 1884, but the hotel's centennial was celebrated in 1983. Ah, well. Wasn't it rather like the elevators stopping on the wrong floor? Or James Farrell having been pronounced dead when he was very much alive? Did it really matter? The grand old building was there; the famous were noted on the plaque; the Chelsea's value had been assessed; and now, as a national monument, it would never be torn down. Arthur Miller, Sandy Daley, Nicholas Quinnell and Charles Jackson had been responsible for that.

I explored the neighbourhood, knowing I was safe for a week or so. It was like the old times when the pimps, patrons of the arts, had arrived to save us. Riss, a greasy-spoon where I had eaten breakfast in the old days, was still there, but there was no more George's Delicatessen and I wondered where Albert had gone, or if he had finally succumbed to a barrage from a Con-Edison man's jackhammer-machine gun. More likely it would be Ripple, Thunderbird or some other horrid form of alcohol. Passing the newspaper kiosk at the corner of Eighth Avenue and Twenty-Third Street, I was hailed by the vendor. It was the same one from my day, older, a little grizzled, but still looking like Gene Kelly.

'Hello!' he called, 'and how's your son?' This after ten years ...

Mildred and I tried a few of the new restaurants which just opened. The area was going up-market. This would please Stanley, but it might change aspects of the hotel. I preferred not to think about it.

In the early 'Seventies, at one of George's parties, there had been a young Texan, pianist and composer. His name was Gerald Busby and he had given his first recital at the age of thirteen in his home town, Tyler, Texas. He was also a part-time actor, appearing in Robert Altman's *A Wedding*; he composed the music for Altman's *Three Women*; composed and performed *Runes*, a dance suite for solo piano which was first performed in Paris with great success and afterwards with equal success on Broadway. In September 1983, Gerald had presented *Busby Music* at Theatre Guinevere in New York, a performance which the *New York Times* called an 'enticing evening of musical theatre', and in which Mildred Baker had appeared in one of the numbers.

Meeting Gerald and his friend, sitting drinking vodka martinis with them and Mildred in Mildred's apartment, I felt better about something that had disturbed me earlier in the day. This was a renovation that Stanley was making where an ominous feeling of Holiday Inn atmosphere had invaded the rooms. They were cheerful, bright, re-decorated, but not the Chelsea. One hoped profoundly that they were not the shape of things to come, a tide from the outside world sweeping the past away.

But if people like Gerald prevailed and inhabitants of long, or even recent, standing also held out, surely there could be no permanent change in the Chelsea. The ambiance was maintained by the inhabitants, and some of the newcomers, like Jonathan Berg, a stockbroker living in Shirley Clarke's old penthouse apartment, appear to understand and wish to be part of the ambiance. I had met him that afternoon with Susan Kleinsinger, when he was busy watering his roses. With a fifteen-year lease and a respect for people who, unlike his clients, are interested in 'things other than making money', he may be a new patron of the arts. One feels that in the current climate of Reaganesque piety the pimps no longer belong.

On the other hand, Allen Ginsberg, drop-out poet and one of the great Beats, has exchanged his prayer shawl for a suit and tie, the result, apparently, of a six-figure contract with Harper for six books of poetry. Happily, a recent photograph in *Time* magazine shows him still using the lotus position. Sartorial change must be incumbent for an imposing bank account. But Allen Ginsberg has been noted for his generosity towards other artists; he deserves this change in fortune.

Once more, the time was coming for me to leave my old home. Other good friends who had also left were Irene, my Southern maid, who had retired; Sandy, living in Brooklyn somewhere, as unavailable as if she had been lost in her native South Dakota mountains. Juliette was in Cleveland, still weaving her wonderful tapestries; Harry was evicted for his inevitable bad behaviour, but I will find him one day if he has not vanished into the hinterlands of America. But whether I see them or not, any of the absent ones, absent by choice or death, a distillation of thought and music, colour and sculpture, will live on in the halls and the rooms, a memorial to the effects of those inspired by and happy within the Hotel Chelsea.

Addendum: One night in 1973, Juliette and I took Juliette's dog Pepe for a run on the roof. Coming back, we sat down for a moment on the top step of the familiar, lovely staircase and listened to the music of the house: a ruffle of piano; distant drums; laughter, suddenly stilled as an elevator door closed.

'Listen.'

Through the quiet hum of the building sounded George's Chinese nightingale, an entrancing pure tumble of song. The moon shone through the big skylight.

'It's full!' I said.

A Stella Waitzkin moon. Moon of witches and witchcraft. Moon inducing madness, the old crazy times of Eliot running through the corridors with flowers in his hair; of Harry loudly playing the Brecht/

Weill song from *Mahagonny*, 'Oh, Moon of Alabama' – 'Show me the way to the next whisky bar'. Full moon at the Chelsea.

As we walked down the stairs, Juliette said, 'You saw a full moon in the skylight but I think, *cherie*, it was only the reflection of an electric light bulb.'